Public S

Workbook,

Public Speaking

Fear

And

Stuttering Help

Beat the Fear of Public Speaking to Go From
Nervousness to Delivering an Engaging Speech
With Confidence and Without Stuttering

By Clark Darsey

Contents

Thank you for buying this book and I hope that you will find it useful. If you will want to share your thoughts on this book, you can do so by leaving a review on the Amazon page, it helps me out a lot.

Public Speaking Workbook

Step by Step Guide to Go From Being Nervous to Confidently Engaging the Audience

By Clark Darsey

Introduction to Public Speaking Workbook

Chapter 1: Introducing Public Speaking

Communication is important in this century. It provides an edge. Public speaking certainly works towards this objective.

The diversity of viewpoints today, which are frequently questionable, has increased the requirement for public speaking. Individuals want to voice out their views to operate properly in society. For thousands of years, public speaking has been the secret to creating and maintaining a democratic society and way of living. Its impacts are large and impact almost all elements of life, like how we think or act. It is additionally utilized in congress, in court proceedings and even in the plain setting of a class.

Speaking in public could often be a genuine hurdle, if not a source of humiliation, not just to regular individuals, but even to individuals of high rank like scholars, medical professionals, artists and business owners. They might have hesitations in dealing with an audience, typically accompanied by stuttering, sweaty palms, and the tip-of-the-tongue phenomenon. These dilemmas typically trigger unknown issues to the speaker (particularly in self-expression) and undesirable effects on the audience.

You most likely got this guide due to the fact that you are up for a speech quickly, and you require important tips. Or possibly, you noticed the connection between success and successful speaking, and have recognized this could assist you. Ideally, this book would do that.

Technical terms in public speaking are described here to assist you in growing as an excellent public speaker.

Cautious thought has been provided to individuals who truly enjoy speaking publicly yet do not have the time to get ready for such. This is going to assist you in making your following speech an excellent one, and progress with every succeeding speech. It intends to assist individuals in writing and delivering an intriguing, clear, and sound speech.

This guide additionally attempts to address the questions and worries of the infrequent speaker.

Included additionally in this guide is a summary of experiences in public speaking, and how they have resulted in success.

Aristotle stated, "a speaker requires 3 qualities-- good character, good sense and goodwill towards his hearers." Therefore, public speaking is additionally about establishing speakers, and eventually, good people.

Whether the speech is long or short, the identical guidelines apply, like the guideline of preparation. The practice of preparation is behind good speakers. Some would state that they talk from "inspiration," when, actually, they have actually been prepping their speeches all their lives.

Chapter 2: Public Speaking and You

Certain individuals are natural speakers. The majority are not. Thus, you are not on your own when you state that you do not delight in holding speeches and speaking before a big audience. Stage fright is unavoidable. Stars are constantly worried to some degree prior to every play.

Possibly you believe your career does not involve public speaking. This is where you're incorrect since regardless of what your job is, public speaking eventually is going to enter into the picture somehow. This chapter, for that reason, concentrates on the importance of public speaking in our everyday lives and on certain particulars of the communication procedure.

4 General Kinds Of Public Speakers

The Avoider

Does all you can to stay away from dealing with an audience. Sometimes, avoiders look for professions which do not consist of making presentations.

The Resister

He ends up being afraid when asked to speak. This worry might be powerful. Resisters might not like to speak in public, however, they don't have a choice. When speaking, they do so with a lot of hesitation.

The Accepter

Can do presentations, however, is not that passionate about doing them. Accepters periodically give presentations and feel great about them. Periodically the presentations could be rather convincing and rewarding.

The Seeker

Constantly tries to find chances to speak. Seekers comprehend that stress and anxiety could be a stimulant which fuels enthusiasm throughout the presentation. Seekers strive to develop their professional communication abilities and self-confidence by speaking frequently.

What Roles Could Public Speaking Have in Your Life?

Public speaking success could open a universe of possibilities for you. It could assist you to dominate brand-new frontiers. It could widen your horizons via personal growth, impact, and advances in your occupation.

1. Public Speaking Improves Your Personal Advancement

In Maslow's hierarchy of needs, recognizing man's self-worth ranks the greatest. Giving speeches assists the speaker to recognize self-worth via the personal fulfillment he experiences whenever a great speech is given. The speaker ends up being more positive, specifically when the audience reacts favorably. It additionally minimizes stress and anxiety when asked by an authority to speak before some individuals.

Once there was a student who dropped a course 5 times since he disliked speaking before the class. Yet after a self-study on developing self-confidence, he chose to give public speaking a shot and succeeded. Actually, he came to take pleasure in the experience and even volunteered to deliver more speeches.

Through public speaking tools such as conceptualization, research, and organization, you have a methodical and successful method of presenting your ideas; and therefore, you are going to have the ability to express yourself much better. You are going to additionally end up being more open to other individuals. In addition, speaking abilities put you in a more considerable role as you talk with individuals of high standing. Finally, public speaking satisfies your feeling of accomplishment when the audience warmly embraces you. This reflects your degree of acumen and communication abilities. All these add to your self-confidence.

2. Public Speaking Impacts Your Society

It is not just you who could gain from communication, but society too. A lot of governments hearken the voice of their people; with appropriate communication abilities, you could represent the public in voicing out your rights and viewpoints.

An instance of this would be a neighborhood discussion. Normally, when a neighborhood holds routine meetings, it talks about specific problems or courses of action. In the discussion, numerous viewpoints are shared, and there you have an apparent public speaking interplay.

Individuals from all over have to speak in public, whether officially or otherwise. From children reciting in school, to people in a town conference, to people voicing out national concerns; from a plain market merchant, to a company president. There is actually no chance you could stay away from public speaking.

3. Public Speaking Advances Your Occupation

Public speaking could assist in your profession, and ultimately, your finances. Typically, success is evaluated by answers to questions like, "How long have you been in your job?" or "Do you hold an MBA degree or something comparable?" Nevertheless, scientists have actually shown that the ideal indication of success in any occupation is whether the individual is frequently asked to hold speeches. Those who deliver more speeches have a tendency to have greater salaries than those who deliver less or no speeches.

Take this typical engineer. She enlists in a public speaking workshop which teaches 2 hours a week for 6 weeks. After 2 months, she is promoted to senior engineer! Her boss has actually been recognizing her outstanding presentations.

The more you work for the company and the more you climb up the organizational ladder, the more your boss is going to ask you to preside over meetings and to deliver talks to the personnel and subordinates or the clients. The higher your position, the more your obligations in leading individuals beneath you, and the more you need to speak successfully.

Aside from huge companies such as General Motors and IBM, little organizations and businesses in the nation additionally require employees who are excellent public speakers. Take the high school coach, for instance. If he is not convincing sufficiently to tell the school board that brand-new gym devices are required, the school athletes may need to bear with the old gym devices.

Similarly, in case parents are not sufficiently convincing when they grumble about a school dress code, their kids might wind up still wearing uniforms in school. If salesmen can not describe their items with an effective sales pitch, then fewer individuals would purchase their products. This is additionally correct for nurses, physicians, firefighters, cops personnel and other occupations. Even General Motors employees frequently meet to make group decisions which they are going to formally present to management.

The bottom line is that whatever roadway you take, you are going to come across occasions that call for you to speak in public.

Chapter 3: Your Initial Speech

Picture that you're in a class. Who do you think speaks wonderfully? You might pick those who appear clever or those who frequently recite in class. You might believe that these individuals are, in fact, more self-assured than you believe they are. Or possibly, they are natural speakers, and you are not.

Well, it might amaze you that they're most likely believing the exact identical thing about you! They might additionally believe that you are a natural speaker and envy you since they have public speaking fears. Some might have special interests in public speaking, however, many folks do not know anything about it.

However, you might, in fact, be an excellent speaker without recognizing it. It pays to discover by really doing it and by seeing yourself doing it. You might be much like this student throughout his initial speech in class.

He had to prepare a lengthy speech. 2 weeks previously, he had actually begun composing his speech. He could not sleep during the night. Actually, the night prior to his speech, he did not sleep whatsoever. Nevertheless, when he lastly delivered his speech and saw it on video, he recognized that it was not as lousy as he anticipated it to be. He did not experience the typical signs of speech anxiety, like going blank during speaking, or speaking extremely gently and hearing chuckles in the audience. Through the video, he found that he has, in fact, gotten better at public speaking.

If no video of your speech is available yet, you could see yourself formally speak before a mirror.

Getting Ready to Speak

Here are the fundamental guidelines of public speaking:

- Understand who you are. Find your own understanding, abilities, predispositions, and capacities.

- Understand your audience. Ponder upon what the audience wishes to hear, what they believe in, what provokes their interest and what they wish to learn.

- Understand the circumstance. Consider how the setting of the location and other unpredicted aspects might impact how you give your speech.

- Expect answers from the audience. Ensure you have an apparent purpose to ensure that the audience is going to react how you desire them to.

- Look for other sources of information. There may be more materials offered for you to make your speech more vibrant.

- Create a reasonable argument. Ensure that the objective of your speech is supported by reliable and clear data to develop a solid argument.

- Include structure to your message. Arrange your ideas to ensure that the audience is not going to have a tough time following and absorbing your ideas.

- Talk straight to your audience. Ensure the language you are utilizing is one which your audience is comfy with. Consider the context of giving your speech.

- Gain confidence with practice. Just with practice could you successfully present your speech. Master your presentation's flow by consistently practicing it. Like that, you could control your speech.

Ending Up Being an Excellent Public Speaker

You have actually most likely heard professors deliver uninteresting and boring lectures. Boring presentations plainly point to the fact that a great deal of individuals do not give much significance to great speeches. These speakers might even be uninformed that they are uninteresting or ineffective since they do not have knowledge about the fundamental qualities of an excellent speech.

For this reason, to prevent this mistake, you need to keep in mind certain fundamental principles.

1. Respect the variety of the audience.

Great speakers do not look down on their audience. They think about the audience as equals. They understand that the listeners have various backgrounds; for this reason, communicating with every one of them successfully would additionally require various techniques.

Prior to really arranging a speech, you need to take into account your audience. Take into consideration things such as gender, age and cultural backgrounds. What do they understand about your subject? What are their values and beliefs? By taking a look at these aspects, you could pick a subject which matches them and design your speech in the way you feel would be most successful.

The entire experience could be more satisfying if you prepare properly for the cultural and individual distinctions of your audience. For instance, are both female and male listeners going to value the information you are going to prepare? Would your Hispanic audience be comfy with the language you're utilizing as much as the Native Americans? Would a few of your remarks upset the elderly people while addressing the younger crowd? The more you understand about the audience, the better the odds that you are going to grab their attention, and you could make your speech fit their circumstances that much more. They would feel comfy hearing you, and you would have a much better interaction.

2. Know as much as you can about listening.

Effective communication does not just depend upon excellent speakers; it depends upon excellent listeners too. It is a two-way street. If the speaker prepares a really refined speech, it would be worthless if the audience does not listen. Know additionally how to "listen" to the gesticulated responses of your audience. How comfy or anxious they appear speaks volumes in regards to their interest or understanding.

3. Arrange thoroughly to enhance recall and understanding.

The ideal presentations are those with interconnected ideas which stream efficiently from one idea to the following. It works due to the fact that the listeners are going to have the ability to follow your arguments and are not going to get perplexed along the road.

3 parts of a well-planned speech:

- Introduction: Grab the your audience's attention, increase their interest, and provide a background of your subject.

- Body: Begin with your main points. Maintain them arranged and support them with verbal and visual aids as much as feasible.

- Conclusion: Supply a wrap-up of all your points and combine them together in a manner that is going to produce an effect on your listeners, making them memorize your points.

4. Utilize language properly.

Maintain it brief. The simpler the language you utilize, the more effective and fascinating your speech is going to be. Too many words expressing a single idea is going to just puzzle the audience and is going to make your argument weak. By keeping it brief but precise, your audience is going to remember what you are going to state, and they are going to value it.

5. Sound natural and passionate.

The issue with first-timers is they either remember the speech verbatim or count on a lot of flashcards for their notes. These could make the speaker sound odd. Talk generally to individuals so they would listen more to you. By being natural and passionate, it would resemble talking about a favorite topic with your buddies. Generally, stay away from putting up a "speaking camouflage" as you talk. Treat it like a normal conversation with your common buddies.

6. Utilize top quality visual aids.

A basic text consisting of crucial expressions and photos is an instance of visual aid. Generally, visual aids (Chapter 10) could be anything which supplements your speech. It is going to considerably assist your listeners in following the flow of your ideas and in comprehending them at a quicker rate. It additionally gives reliability to your speech, and that makes you feel more unwinded and confident during. Nevertheless, stay away from making bad visuals due to the fact that they end up being more of a diversion than assistance. Deal with visual preparations with equivalent value as the speech preparation itself.

7. Give just ethical speeches.

Precision is extremely crucial. It would be tough for your audience to make educated choices if the information you provide is incorrect or unclear.

Research to ensure clarity and credibility. Stay away from plagiarism, exaggeration and falsification of your information. Additionally, when attempting to persuade, do not manipulate, trick, push, or pressure. Establish great arguments through sound reasoning and concrete proof. This is an ethical persuasion. As soon as information is falsified, it ends up being dishonest due to the fact that it stops listeners from making educated choices.

Essentially, great speakers intend to alter the values, beliefs, or mindsets of the audience through clean persuasion.

Chapter 4: Establishing Speaker Confidence

Regardless of how experienced and interested we might be in public speaking, stress and anxiety can not be stayed away from. We experience it, specifically as the day of the speech gets nearer. We begin to ask questions which make our stomachs churn. For instance: Is the audience going to like me? Is my mind going to go blank when I start to speak? Have I prepared properly?

If the idea of giving a speech makes you worried, you are not on your own! Based upon a typically quoted survey, more individuals are scared of public speaking than they are of death. Individuals who experience a lot of apprehension while speaking are at a disadvantage compared to more confident, conversational individuals.

People who express themselves confidently are deemed more proficient. They additionally produce a better impression throughout job interviews and are more probable to be promoted than anxious individuals.

Self-confidence establishes a positive impression, while stress and anxiety develop a negative one. When we talk, we are communicating in 3 ways - visually, verbally, and vocally. Our verbal delivery might be clear and well arranged, however, when we are anxious, the audience is going to probably detect more of our unfavorable visual and vocal indications (for instance, absence of eye contact, bad posture, reluctant delivery, and strained vocal quality). However, when we are confident and our visual, verbal, and vocal signals remain in unity, we appear more reputable.

If we want individuals to trust us when we talk, if we wish to enhance the impressions we make, we want to increase our self-confidence. This chapter is going to provide you with some pointers on how to handle speech anxiety to deliver more professional and confident deliveries.

Name it stage fright, speech anxiety, or communication apprehension; you need to comprehend it for various reasons. Initially, speech anxiety could paralyze you. Second, misunderstandings about it could enhance your anxiety. Lastly, understanding the methods for handling speech anxiety could assist in decreasing your apprehension.

Factors Adding To Speech Anxiety

Speech anxiety isn't anything new-- it's been around for as long as individuals have actually been speaking with one another. A lot of speakers who have actually experienced speech anxiety understand the significance of being confident and calm when talking.

Certain folks feel anxious, while others remain calm and kicked back when talking. Factors in speech anxiety vary from individual to individual. However, basic elements apply to everybody.

Understanding the reasons for speech anxiety is the primary step in handling it successfully. Numerous anxiety-generating elements impact almost all of us, including:

- Poor preparation

- Unsuitable self-expectations

- Worry of assessment

- Too much self-focusing

- Fear of the audience

- Not comprehending our body's responses

Misunderstandings about Speech Anxiety

Nobody would concur that experiencing speech anxiety is satisfying. Nevertheless, when we better acknowledge why our bodies react as they do, we end up being more ready to face our anxieties.

Let us analyze some misunderstandings and how to counter them.

Misconception: Everybody is going to know if a speaker has speech anxiety.

Truth: A couple of people, if any, are going to notice. So keep the secret to yourself and begin acting self-assured.

Misconception: Speech anxiety is going to magnify as the speech advances.

Truth: It's all up to you. Mainly, a well-prepared speaker is going to unwind as the speech advances.

Misconception: Speech anxiety is going to mess up the impact of the speech.

Truth: If you allow it, it is going to. On the contrary, speech anxiety might enhance a speaker's performance.

Misconception: The audience is naturally hostile and is going to be extremely critical of what we do.

Truth: Many listeners are respectful, specifically when the speaker is clearly attempting to do good.

Methods for Handling Speech Anxiety

Each speaker needs to understand the various techniques offered for handling speech anxiety. As you give speeches, you discover techniques that work, particularly for you. Let's take a look at some methods which have actually been extremely helpful for lots of speakers.

1. Practice Your Speech and Be Ready.

Absolutely nothing could make you feel more distressed than understanding that you are not ready. Besides, isn't your anxiety everything about looking foolish before your audience? Poor preparation is going to ensure this.

To prepare effectively, initially, attempt to understand your listeners ahead of time (if you can) and arrange your visual aids and speech for this particular group.

Next, have easy-to-follow notes. Utilizing these notes, practice your speech 3 or more times from beginning to end-- speaking up louder every time. Psychologically analyzing your speech is not the identical thing as really speaking before the audience. For example, if you are going to be standing throughout your speech, stand while practicing. If you are going to be utilizing visual aids, practice utilizing them. When you practice, time yourself to see if you need to shorten or extend the speech.

Last but not least, anticipate feasible questions and have answers for them. Understanding that you are ready is going to assist in decreasing a lot of your apprehension.

2. Warm Up First.

Speakers are similar to singers who warm up their voices, artists who warm up their fingers, or professional athletes who warm up their muscles prior to a performance. Prior to delivering a speech, you'll want to warm up your voice and loosen your muscles. Different methods can assist you in doing this. For example, attempt singing up and down the scale, the way singers do prior to a show. Read aloud a page from a book or a note, altering your volume, rate, pitch, and quality. Do a bit of stretching workouts like rolling your head from side to side and touching your toes. Practice various gestures like pounding your fist, pointing, or shrugging your shoulders. Much like artists and professional athletes, these warm-up exercises are going to assist you to unwind and are going to make certain that you are ready to present at your finest.

3. Utilize Deep Breathing.

One quick way to soothe your anxiety is with deep breathing. This includes inhaling deep breaths through the nose, holding it as you count to 5, and after that gradually breathing out through your mouth. As you breathe out, think that the pressure and uneasiness is gradually draining out your fingertips and down your arms and down your body and legs and out your toes. Redo the procedure a 2nd or 3rd time if needed.

4. Prepare an Introduction Which Is Going To Relax Your Audience and You.

The majority of speakers discover that as soon as they get a beneficial audience response, they are going to relax. This is why a number of speakers start with humor-- it relaxes their audience and them. If a funny introduction is not appropriate or you are uneasy with humor, sharing the private experience is another option. Whatever you choose, make your preliminary moves work so you could feel comfy during your speech.

5. Concentrate on Meaning.

Instead of fretting about how you sound or look, or about whether you impress your listeners, concentrate your energy on getting your meaning across to your audience. To put it simply, make certain your listeners are following the order of your speech and comprehending your concepts. Pay attention to their nonverbal feedback. In case they appear puzzled, describe the idea once again or add another instance. A speaker who is concentrating on the audience quickly forgets about being anxious.

6. Utilize Visual Aids.

Visual aids make listening simpler for your audience and boosts your self-confidence. They make it virtually inconceivable for you to forget your main points. If you're not sure of the following point, simply set up your following visual aid. Additionally, utilizing visual aids like flipcharts, posters, or actual items don't just add captivating motions to your presentation. They can additionally keep you totally engaged in your discussion, so you are going to be troubled less by your look.

7. Establish a Positive Mental Attitude.

With positive imagery, you establish a positive, vibrant, and comprehensive mental image of yourself. When you picture yourself speaking with confidence, you end up being more confident. In your mind, you could mimic sensations (of pride, for example) even when no actual circumstance exists. Certainly, positive imagery alone is not going to provide you the result you desire unless you practice your speech and prepare.

Positive self-imagery could be utilized in lots of elements of life. It could assist us in handling apprehension in problem-solving discussions, job interviews, testing circumstances, or any situations in which our self-confidence requires a boost.

To prosper in public speaking, you need to imagine yourself as an effective speaker. No quantity of encouragement, talk, or practice is going to make you effective if you deem yourself as a nervous or ineffective speaker.

Chapter 5: Conquering Your Fear

You are going to benefit at the start of your speech if you free yourself from 2 mistaken beliefs:

1. Successful speakers are born, not made; it is futile to attempt being one if you were not blessed with God-given capability.

2. For the majority of folks, fear and anxiety are inconceivable to get rid of; it is worthless even to attempt.

Let's have a look at every one of these incorrect assumptions.

Are Excellent Speakers Born and Not Made?

You do not really believe this, or you would not be holding this guide. Everybody is born a baby, and babies can't speak. The "born speaker" misconception is an alibi for not trying. Individuals who believe it just wish to save their faces from the disgrace speech mistake might bring. It is a truth that practice makes perfect.

A speaker is one who talks to other people with a purpose. When you were 2 or 3 years of age and initially said, "Mommy, I want a glass of water," you were delivering a speech. In fact, you have actually been making speeches from the time you were able to talk.

You could end up being a great speaker in case you have these tools:

1. A voice.

2. Standard language construction: i.e., working grammar and vocabulary.

3. A thing to say.

4. A desire to share your ideas with others.

You have actually been utilizing these tools for many years. You have actually been saying something to others a number of times each day, and under these conditions, you call it "conversation." The conversation is speaking to a few. Public speaking is, basically, speaking with a bigger group.

Your audience is simply a group of people. You could talk quickly with a couple of people. So simply think of public speaking as speaking with people all at the same time - or speaking with the group as to a single person.

Can You Overcome Fear?

There are 3 options to assist you to minimize fear and make it work for you rather than versus you:

1. Accept it as nature's method of aiding you.

You do not have to be frightened of fear when you embrace it as nature's method of shielding you and assisting you. Acknowledge it. Do not condemn yourself for having it. All of us feel fear. Whether your fear comes from the idea of standing alone on your own on stage before numerous individuals, and even from the idea of getting upstage to speak, remember that you are reacting ordinarily.

Professional athletes are nervous prior to a crucial competition; artists shiver prior to a concert; entertainers feel stage fright. Skilled speakers never ever eliminate apprehension prior to speaking, nor do they wish to. A knowledgeable star once stated: "I used to have butterflies in my stomach each time I stood before an audience. Now that I understand how to make them work for me, they fly in formation."

Understanding that you are subject to an ordinary and typical human reaction, you could drive out the greatest element adding to your fear: You could quit condemning yourself for being uncommon.

Psychologists tell us that fear is not an actual obstacle. We feel uncomfortable or useless since we believe fear is wrong. It is not fear itself yet your sensation about it that dissatisfies you. Franklin

Roosevelt's note on the speech of Henry Thoreau sums it up: "We have absolutely nothing to fear but fear itself." As quickly as you understand this and acknowledge it, you are on the path to self-mastery.

Fear is a natural method of preparing you for danger, genuine or imagined. When you deal with a brand-new situation, or when many folks are viewing you, and you do not wish to mess up, nature does something terrific to assist you if you acknowledge the assistance instead of being dissatisfied with it. Nature brings in adrenaline in your bloodstream. It accelerates your pulse and your reactions. It boosts your blood pressure to alert you. It supplies you with the additional energy you require to do your finest. Without anxiety, there would be no additional effort. Recognize fear as a buddy. Acknowledge it and utilize it properly.

2. Evaluate Your Fear.

Your following step in mastering fear is effortless and easy. Evaluate your kind of fear. Fear is a tool for safety. What are you shielding? You are stressed over your self-esteem. In public speaking, there are just 3 threats to self-esteem:

(a) Fear of yourself-- fear of choking up or not pleasing your self-esteem.

(b) Fear of your audience-- fear they might tease or make fun of you.

(c) Fear of your material-- fear you have absolutely nothing reasonable to say or you are not properly prepared.

Fear of yourself (a) and fear of your audience (b) are quite linked. It is feasible to be pleasing yourself while falling short of fulfilling your audience. Going for audience approval is typically a much better option since, if you are successful, you are, actually, additionally pleasing yourself.

However, in aspiring to please your audience, you should never ever jeopardize your message. Often you might need to deliver a message to individuals you understand are especially opposed to it. This requires guts. Do not fear to disagree. Excellent speakers have actually done so and have actually happily strolled off the stage effectively. Sincere beliefs equip a speaker and deliver power to the speech.

3. Utilize what you have learned.

You now understand that fear, nature's ace in the hole, can really assist you to be successful. You found you were not actually scared of fear yet of your audience, of yourself, and your material. Now, utilize your knowledge. Here's how:

a. Conceal your negative feelings from other people. If you do not have confidence, conceal it. Allowing the audience to know it will not assist you in any way. Never ever discuss it. This is going to simply make you feel even worse. Act with confidence. It is going to rub off on you. You are going to look how you feel. Ever heard of the frightened young boy who walked past the cemetery one night? As long as he walked delicately and whistled happily, he was fine. However, when he walked quicker, he might not decline the urge to run; and when he ran, fear took over.

Do not give up. Remain relaxed and calm. Have fun with your audience and your talk.

b. Examine your condition fairly. Think about the reasons why you were called to speak. Among other feasible speakers, you were picked. Whoever asked you had faith in you, or you would not have actually been selected.

You are considered a skilled, great speaker. And you understand your subject. You understand more about it than your listeners do.

Your assessment exposes that you are ready to succeed and that you have the advantage over your listeners. If you accept this, your self-confidence is going to show to your audience. It is going to make them trust in your speech and in you.

c. Examine your audience fairly. They want you to succeed. Listeners suffer together with a speaker who is having trouble delivering, and they do not take pleasure in suffering. They would prefer to criticize and react; that would give them a great time. So consider your audience instead of yourself. Win their interest, and you are going to have more confidence, and everyone is going to be happy.

One more way of putting this: Concentrate on speech delivery and an excellent message. You are going to make the audience delighted with this, and you are going to be successful in your objective. Do the first properly, and the second is going to follow.

d. Evaluate your material fairly. Fear of speech material is the simplest to overcome, given that the answer is easy: preparation and knowledge. Preparation and knowledge eliminate fear, however, on their own, they do not instantly guarantee the delivery of an effective speech.

An excellent start is when you acknowledge you do not have to be scared-- of yourself, your material or your audience. And as you be successful in creating speeches, you are going to quickly say, "I can do it since I have done it so many times."

9 Fundamental Steps in Preparing Your Speech

1. Pick your subject.

2. Identify your specific purpose.

3. Determine your speech objective/s.

4. Examine your audience.

5. Plan and arrange your main points.

6 Arrange your introduction and conclusion.

7. Have an outline.

8. Have your visual aids successfully.

9. Rehearse your speech.

Chapter 6: Picking Your Subject

In certain circumstances, speakers are provided a particular subject. However, the majority of the time, you are going to be provided a basic kind of speech with the option of a particular subject left up to you. As soon as you have actually determined what kind of speech you are going to be making, follow these guidelines in selecting a particular subject:

- Pick a subject you currently understand a great deal about. You are going to feel a lot more relaxed and positive speaking about a thing you know about rather than checking out the Reader's Digest and choosing a subject which you don't know anything about.

- Select a subject you have an interest in going over. You might understand a great amount about numerous subjects, however, you might not be extremely interested in them. Stay away from these subjects. It is difficult to interest the audience in a topic which does not interest you.

- Select a subject which you could make intriguing and/or beneficial to your listeners. Your audience does not need to have an interest in your subject before you speak, however, they need to be when you are done speaking. If you examine your prospective listeners, you need to have a rather decent comprehension of their interests.

- Select a subject that fits the requirements of the task. Make certain you understand the kind of speech, the time restraints, and any other requirements, and select your subject appropriately.

You might additionally wish to perform a self-inventory to aid you think of feasible subjects. Ask yourself the following:

- What are my educational and intellectual interests?

- What do I love to read?

- What fascinating things have I learned from tv?

- What specific courses, or subjects covered in courses, have particularly interested me?

- What are my career objectives? What do I want to do with my life?

- What are my favorite interests and leisure activities? What things do I do for entertainment that other people may wish to find out more about or participate in?

- What private and social issues are notable to me?

- What is happening in my life that troubles or impacts me?

- What is occurring beyond my instant world that is in need of improvement?

Narrowing Down the Subject

When you have actually selected your basic subject, you are prepared to narrow it down based on your listener's interests and requirements. Here are the actions to follow in narrowing down a subject:

1. Pick prospective speech subjects (from self-inventory).

2. Think about situational aspects.

- Familiarity: Are my listeners going to be familiar with any information that is going to assist me in picking a subject?

- Current events: Can I choose a subject to highlight present events which may be of considerable interest to my audience?

- Audience apathy: Could I motivate my audience to be less apathetic towards events which are important to me?

- Time frame: Do I have ample time to go over the subject adequately?

3. Think about audience elements.

- Prior knowledge: What do my listeners currently know?

- Typical experiences: What typical experiences have my listeners come across?

- Common interests: Where do my interests and my listeners' interests meet?

- Appropriate diverse elements: How diverse are my listeners?

4. Pick your tentative subject.

Certain instances of narrowing down might be seen beneath:

GENERAL SUBJECT: Career Choices

NARROWED DOWN: career choices of graduates of leading American schools

NARROWED DOWN FURTHER: career choices of graduates of leading American schools in the previous 5 years

NARROWED DOWN EVEN FURTHER: elements impacting the career choices of MBA graduates of Wharton School of Business in the previous 5 years

GENERAL SUBJECT: Southeast Asia

NARROWED DOWN: security issues in Southeast Asia

NARROWED DOWN FURTHER: roots of terrorism in Southeast Asia

NARROWED DOWN EVEN FURTHER:
cooperation amongst governments of Southeast
Asia in attending to the issues of terrorism

GENERAL SUBJECT: Real Estate

NARROWED DOWN: housing projects in the last
ten years

NARROWED DOWN FURTHER: housing projects
in City X.

NARROWED DOWN EVEN FURTHER: funding
issues in the housing projects in City X.

Identifying Your Precise Objective.

The fundamental objectives of public speaking are
to inform, to teach, to amuse, and to persuade.
These 4 are not mutually exclusive of each other. A
speaker might have numerous objectives in mind. It
might be to inform and additionally to amuse.
Another speaker might wish to inform and,
simultaneously, persuade. Even though
organization, content, and delivery might have 2 or
more objectives, many have simply one main
objective.

Speeches which inform offer precise data, unbiased information, findings, and occasionally, analyses of these findings. Those that inform teach the audience a procedure or a process based upon information offered in the speech. Those who entertain offer enjoyment and pleasure which make the audience smile or identify with wonderful circumstances. Lastly, speeches which persuade attempt to persuade the audience to take a specific stand on a problem, a belief, or an idea, by appealing initially to reason via logical arguments and proof, and to the feelings by moving claims.

Determining the Goals of the Speech

A goal is more restricted and particular. It might target habits or thoughts. What does the message communicated in the speech hope to achieve? What reaction does it welcome from the audience? Does it wish to persuade the listeners to support a cause by signing up with a movement? Does it want the listeners to purchase a specific item or utilize a particular service? Does it want the listeners to customize their habits via a process provided? Does it wish to move the listeners to laughter and later on to reflection on a considerable social concern? Does it wish to supply precise and reputable information to lead them to a decision? As responses to these questions are provided, speech goals could be determined and stated.

Here are certain instances:

Subject: A Call for Support for Dependence of Old Age

Objective: to persuade

Goal/s: The speech is going to look for pledges of time, effort, or cash to aid in establishing an institution to support the dependency of old age.

Subject: Why My Objective in Life Is to End Up Being an Attorney

Objective: to educate

Goal/s: After hearing my speech, the audience is going to comprehend why my dream is to end up being an attorney.

Chapter 7: Evaluating Your Audience

The more you understand about your audience, the more you are going to be able to link your subject to them. Audience analysis is easy. It generally calls for understanding your audience well so you could arrange your visual, verbal, and vocal delivery to fit their scenarios. When examining an audience, you aren't attempting to trick, control, or force them; you are simply making certain your speech fits them and maintains them interested.

Speeches have to be centered on audience, so audience analysis is a must. Presentation design-- content, organization, and delivery-- is affected by the sort of audience expected at the presentation, so make certain they comprehend the significance and implication of the message. For effectiveness, a speaker ought to understand the following:

1. Who are the listeners?

Attempt to remember the basic age range, male-female ratio, academic background, profession or occupation, race, ethnic background, religious beliefs, cultural or geographical environment, civil status, income level and assets, organizational and group subscriptions.

2. What do they desire from you?

Are they there to get directions? Do they want the present problems explained? Do they additionally wish to have a good time? Do they require information? Have they come on their own, or were they required to attend?

Voluntary audiences are most probable to be homogeneous; they have things in common. Classroom students comprise an involuntary audience; they are heterogeneous. They differ in numerous ways.

3. What is the audience size?

How big is the audience? Is it an audience of 20 or 200? In a classroom, you would be talking to approximately thirty pupils. However, in other settings, you might be talking to a tinier group (such as a buzz group) or a larger group (such as a rally).

Audience size might contribute to anxiety and might impact speech delivery, more so in using visual aids, the kind of language you utilize, and so on. In general, you wish to talk more formally with bigger groups.

4. Where is the location of the presentation?

Is the location going to be a room? What type of room is it going to be - a meeting room, a hall maybe, or a little meeting room?

When speaking in a classroom, you are speaking in a familiar, comfy setting. You understand whether the lights could be dimmed, there is an overhead projector, etc.

As you do speeches, you are going to discover more about other settings for public speaking, such as outdoor stages, or shopping centers and hotel lounges. You might be curious to understand how it feels speaking while standing at the floor level. Make an effort to find out about podiums, technological assistance, microphones, the sound system, etc.

Audience analysis could be done prior to the presentation, though a lot of times, it occurs throughout the presentation. A sensitive speaker gets a good deal of information from listeners as the talk is being delivered. Typically, the hints are nonverbal, like facial expressions, uneasiness, passiveness, attentiveness, or apathy. When these indications show, he could be sufficiently flexible to change or modify to do a much better task. Shifting gestures, places, voice modifications, or perhaps even audience participation could prove to be helpful.

Here's an instance of audience analysis:

Subject: A Call for Assistance for Dependence of Old Age

Objective: To Persuade

Goal/s: The speech is going to look for pledges of time, effort, or cash to assist in developing an institution to support the dependency of old age.

Audience Analysis:

1. Who the listeners are?

- Heads/officers of religious, civic and business communities in the city

- Nearly equivalent ratio of professional men and women, with high academic achievements and high earning capacity, leaders in their particular fields, mainly Christian audience with 70% Catholics, 80% wed, American and American-Chinese, some Asians.

- Active in civic and social works

- In touch with present social, political, and religious problems

- In touch with prevalent government and business circumstances

2. What do they desire from you?

- Essentially interested in a subject which pertains to their organization or group.

- To get additional information about the dependency of old age, and to understand more about what the speaker will request/propose

- Want enough bases to choose whether or not to support

- Came in response to an official invite

3. What is the audience size?

- 50 individuals

4. Where is the presentation location?

- Medium case room with fixed upholstered seats in a semi-circle

- 2-ft elevation before the speaker

- Great acoustics

- Electronic tools for presentations

Chapter 8: Speech Organization

A great deal of speakers carefully select their subjects, pick a concrete objective, search for excellent supporting resources, and yet never ever experience success in public speaking. It might be partially as a result of bad luck, however, it is mainly attributable to how they have actually laid out and arranged their ideas.

It is like composing an essay. You want to begin with a thesis and choose the main points which are going to clarify or establish it. Organizing, for that reason, is specifying the thesis of the speech and noting down the main points that are going to be utilized to support it.

THE REMEMBER BOX

Presentation organisation has 3 parts: the introduction, body, and conclusion. It is a thesis established with help points. Discourse markers and transition tools connect the parts together.

Organizing the Introduction

The start of your speech is necessary. It offers your audience their initial impression of your topic, objective, and bottom line. However, your start needs to do more than aid them to comprehend your speech. It needs to grab their interest additionally. It is not adequate to state, "Today, I will discuss why the school requires a brand-new basketball gym." It's hard to captivate the audience utilizing this claim. The intro has to be planned to ensure that listeners wish to take notice of your speech, consider you as a trustworthy speaker, and have some idea of your speech's focus and goal.

A great deal of excellent speeches fail due to their complicated and dull introduction. If you do not get off to an excellent start, then odds are, your audience might "tune you out," like a radio listener who just switches channels to get rid of ridiculous programs. Even if individuals sit as part of the audience does not imply they plan to listen-- unless you make it impossible for them not to.

The successful introduction consists of seizing your audience's attention. When you get up to speak, the audience is going to offer you their complete attention typically. However, that attention is short. Beneath are methods of keeping the audience's attention:

- Establish commonalities. Listeners are more probable to pay attention to speakers with whom they have common experiences, issues, or objectives.

- A shocking statement or fact. Utilize interesting or stunning statements or stats which arouse interest. For instance, "950,000 individuals in the Middle East might not have the ability to consume 3 meals a day in the year x." or "Dinosaurs aren't extinct. Whenever you see a songbird, you're looking at a survivor from the Paleozoic period."

- A story or a short anecdote. A fascinating story-- whether it is psychological, funny, perplexing, or appealing-- commands attention. The story could be true or imagine. It could be a private experience, or it could be something you have actually read. For instance, "An intriguing thing occurred on my path here today." or "The initial time I jumped out of an airplane ...".

- A rhetorical or real question. Rhetorical questions do not seek instant answers. Rather, they are targeted to get the audience thinking about a problem or idea. For instance, "Did you know that you lose 10 billion skin cells daily?".

- A quote. You could utilize the words of a well-known entertainer, author, professional athlete, or singer, or other distinguished and highly prestigious figure to get the audience's attention and interest right away. For instance, "When I was a kid, I heard a wise man say ...".

- Utilize humor. Certain speakers like to begin a speech with a funny story, however, you need to manage humor with care. Despite how funny a story is, it needs to be suitable to the point you wish to make. Simply telling a couple of jokes is not a great method to launch a speech, and a joke which fails is embarrassing. Humor must never ever be disrespectful and must never ever be meant to mock somebody or something, so you need to be careful.

You could utilize numerous of the above all at once. For example, you may tell a fascinating story that additionally establishes commonalities and ignites interest.

Stopping briefly after telling an engaging story, asking a rhetorical question, or sharing a remarkable quote might assist audience members to reflect on what you will state. The essential element here is catching and preserving the listeners' attention and interest.

A good introduction gets attention and produces an audience's interest in the subject. It additionally develops suitable expectations by preparing the listeners to get the message. What 3 distinct parts comprise the introduction?

a) The opener-- This is the initial sentence. It could be a quote, a surprising statement or figure, or a short anecdote. This opening ought to be short, intriguing, and proper to the subject.

b) The subject-- This is just specifying the title of the speech. State it directly as: "I have been asked to discuss _____." or "I have picked to talk to you about

_____."

c) The program-- This briefly describes your points of view or what you are going to be talking about.

Here is an instance of an introduction:

(1) Good afternoon, everybody.

(2) It's a delight to be here with you now.

(3) I have actually been asked to introduce myself and been provided 5 minutes to do this.

(4) There is very little I could tell you about myself during that length of time; so, what I am going to do rather is to begin with my subject, which is The

Increasing Participation of Ladies in Social Issues Today.

(5) I feel really highly that ladies' answer to present social problems is evident in, one, how she handles domesticity and home, two, her participation or support of community-based groups for change, and three, her participation in nationwide problems through a more powerful feeling of awareness of these problems.

Sentences 1-3 are the openers, sentence 4 is the subject and sentence 5 is the program.

Effectively, the introduction is short, direct, and ought to get the audience's attention while getting them ready for what is next. In an intriguing way, an introduction plainly sets up the subject and sets a guide on what the audience could anticipate from the speech.

Organizing the Body

At this moment, you're set to arrange your main points and supply verbal and visual aids. The speech's body is its meat, and you ought to put the significant points you wish to expound in this part of your speech. These main points ought to be easy, declarative sentences so that they are quickly acknowledged and remembered when individuals leave your speech. These points require help, clarification, elaboration, and proof. These could come in the type of particular and concrete details, contrasts, instances, and illustrations.

There are a number of actions you may carry out to make your main points unforgettable:

1. Restrict yourself to no more than 3 to 5 main points.

2. Keep your main points short and utilize parallel structures when you can.

3. Organize your material to ensure that you cover your essential point, either first or last.

4. Make your main points unforgettable by producing your own acronym or rhyme when feasible.

Organizing the Conclusion

A great deal of speakers do not, in fact, conclude their speeches-- they simply stop talking. Others might fail at their concluding paragraph, reducing the success of the speech.

The concluding paragraph is necessary. It slowly ushers the audience back to a general evaluation of the discussion. Obviously, a good discussion is going to provide the speaker with more freedom to formulate a conclusion.

No speech is done without a concluding remark, given that the conclusion makes sure all ideas were comprehended and remembered. It offers the required closure. It's probable that certain folks may have missed, have misconstrued, or have actually forgotten a point (possibly they were unfocused or they were fantasizing for a while). Without a conclusion, we can not remedy these issues. A conclusion is additionally important since listeners like and require closure. Without it, they might seem like vacationers left adrift after a pleasure cruise-- a lot of the pleasure produced by the cruise is lost.

The conclusion is especially substantial if you have a question-and-answer period at the final portion of the speech. Offer a quick summary prior to the question-and-answer and another one after it to tie up any loose ends and to reroute attention back to the primary points provided in your speech.

But like the start, the ending ought to be reasonably short, ideally no more than one-seventh of the entire speech. The majority of tools recommended for beginnings are suitable for endings. The shorter you make your ending, the more strong it is going to appear to your audience, and the more quickly they are going to remember it.

Here are certain methods for making good conclusions:

1. Sum up what you have actually said to your audience-- your main ideas and points.

2. Issue a challenge to your audience.

3. Make an appeal for action to your audience.

4. Imagine the future.

5. Add unforgettable quotes.

6. Refer to the introduction, i.e., return the audience to your opening declaration.

Considering that conclusions are so vital and possibly unforgettable, they ought to (1) be quick, (2) never ramble, (3) not present brand-new information, and (4) be built thoroughly. As you are able to see, the conclusion is too important to ignore. If you make your conclusion cautiously, then you are going to end your speech with a tactical close and create a lasting impact.

In case you notice that time is running out, do not get rid of your conclusion. It is better to lessen your last point (or perhaps leave it out totally) than to omit your conclusion. If you time your speech while practicing, you will not need to be troubled about time issues. The time to conclude is when the audience desires more and not when the speaker has actually tired them.

Chapter 9: Outlining Your Speech

What is your response the second you hear the word outline? If your immediate response is a negative one, maybe you have never, in fact, discovered how to outline appropriately, or perhaps your prior writing experiences have actually re-established less-than-ideal memories. Whichever the reason, you are not on your own-- a great deal of individuals dislike outlining. This hatred is regrettable since, when used effectively, outlines could save you a lot of time and could assist you in establishing a considerably better speech.

Fundamental Outlining Principles

Outlining is not going to just assist you in seeing the basic idea of your speech. It is going to additionally assist you in subdividing the message body into sub-topics based upon the order of their significance. Outlining constantly aids - in some cases a bit, in some cases a lot-- yet it constantly aids.

I. What Is an Outline?

A. An outline is a note-taking system which demonstrates how someone has actually arranged a group of ideas.

B. It additionally demonstrates how these ideas relate to each other.

II. Steps To Follow When Outlining

A. Try to find the essential idea or the main point.

1. You ought to write this as a title or thesis declaration.

2. Think in precise terms when outlining.

B. Look for significant ways to subdivide or establish the main point. (This is going to offer you with the significant headings of your outline.) Think about transition words or signals to signify:

1. Chronological order

2. Enumeration.

3.Cause-effect relationships.

4. General to specific/easy to hard.

5.Comparison-contrast.

C.Try to stress details.

1. Stress what you believe is necessary or complex and in need of a more comprehensive explanation.

2. Constantly attempt to link these details to the significant points.

III.Notation In Outlining.

A. The size of the notation and the indentation utilized are identified by the value of the idea.

1. The most essential or main ideas are positioned to the farthest left and are noted with Roman numerals (I, II, III, and so on).

2. The following crucial ideas (the significant details) are put beneath the main ideas and are noted with uppercase (A, B, C, and so on).

3. The small details are put to the right beneath the significant details and are noted with plain numbers (1, 2, 3, and so on).

B. All ideas of the identical significance ought to have equivalent indention, with all significant or main points being designated with roman numerals and being farthest to the left.

C. You might write items in an outline as either expressions or sentences, however, the whole outline ought to be one or the other. Simply put, do not mix expressions and sentences in an identical outline.

D. Always capitalize the initial word of every item in an outline.

E. Constantly position a period after every notation sign (letters and numbers) in an outline.

IV. What are the Outlining Benefits?

A. It is simpler to recognize issues.

B. It is less tough to request for practical assessments.

C. There is less temptation to remember your speech.

D. Flexibility is greater.

Chapter 10: Preparing Your Visual Aids Successfully

Among the simplest approaches to ensure an effective and successful speech is to utilize intriguing and effective visual aids. Regrettably, a great deal of speakers either do not utilize visual whatsoever or utilize difficult-to-read, overcrowded visuals which make it nearly inconceivable for the audience to comprehend the visuals' content, to listen to the talk, and to ditch the notes completely. Inadequately developed visual aids force listeners to choose between listening to the speaker or reading the visual aid-- and you understand which they are going to choose. Hence, when preparing your visuals, bear in mind that if listeners are going to take a lot longer than 7 seconds to understand the content, they are going to fall into a reading mode potentially. When listeners are thrown inside a reading mode, they hear practically nothing the speaker says.

Audiovisual aids might be utilized to enhance, describe, or additionally clarify the primary points. These aids vary from basic flipcharts or charts to slides or videos. Communication effectiveness is regularly boosted by the utilization of more than one medium, and when the presenter selects visual aids, they need to show the relevance of their usage to the message.

Function of Visual Aids

Visual aids, when utilized successfully, could assist a speaker in communicating much better and could assist listeners to comprehend better. Visual aids engage the senses (what we hear and see) and assist in clarifying, supporting, and enhancing the message. Visual aids are so successful that many speakers utilize them.

Let's think about how visual aids could enhance your presentation. Visual aids are able to:

- offer assistance and stress main points

- help with understanding

- promote emotional involvement

- aid with delivery

- contribute to your credibility

- reduce your anxiety since they offer you a thing to do with your hands, they draw the audience's attention far from you, and they render it nearly inconceivable to forget what you wish to say.

Listeners additionally gain from the successful utilization of visual aids. Such aids could:

- aid to separate essential from the less important

- include color and interest

- enhance audience memory

Chapter 11: Delivering Your Message Successfully

After all the preparations which enter into your speech, you ultimately present yourself to the audience. You might have spent days or perhaps weeks to examine your possible listeners, choose your subject, arrange and practice your speech. However, you are going to complete your speech delivery in simply a couple of minutes. Nonetheless, real delivery is the highlight and end of the public speaking experience.

Delivery is among the most apparent aspects of public speaking, and one which brings in the preliminary attention of both the audience and the speaker.

If one were to ask a listener what he thought about a speech which had actually simply been delivered, the reply would be something like: "I believe she has an extremely enjoyable voice;" "I believe he ought to have walked around more;" and "I could not always hear her."

Certainly, delivery is not all in public speaking. A great delivery can not make up for an improperly prepared message, or one without substance. In spite of that, the majority of us understand the significance of delivery, and sometimes it frightens us. We might feel quite at ease getting the speech ready, performing the research, arranging and outlining our ideas, etc. Nevertheless, when confronted with the real "standing and delivering," we might end up being really worried. The more we understand about delivery, the much better our odds of doing it effectively. Delivery might not be all in speech development, however, it is an extremely apparent and vital part.

Take, for example, the case of a well-known talk-show host - Oprah Winfrey. Oprah's program still leads the talk-show rankings. How does she do it? She is passionate, fascinating, effective, convincing, caring, and-- most importantly-- credible. She looks like if she is speaking straight to each of her audience; she is genuine, and she is credible. She does more than simply arranging persuading ideas; she provides her ideas in a credible way. She understands how to get in touch with her audience by interacting with them visually, verbally, and vocally.

Your delivery isn't more important than what you have to say, however without great delivery, your listeners might never ever hear what you have to say. To make your presentation credible, you need to practice.

Visual Delivery

Due to the fact that the initial impression stems more from what the audience sees than from what they hear, we are going to initially speak about visual delivery-- especially how to appear to your audience. As a speaker, your physical look, posture, eye contact, facial expressions, body language, and gestures all affect your audience's perception.

The audience judges your look as a tip to your position, trustworthiness, and knowledge. Unless you are certain about what is appropriate for the audience and the event, the best thing to do is to dress conservatively.

Excellent posture is absolutely nothing more than standing directly and having your "chest out" and "stomach in." Appropriate posture makes the speaker feel and look comfortable and helps with poise and voice projection.

Walk around sometimes. Body language could include energy, interest, and self-confidence in your presentation. To include emphasis, attempt moving at the start of an idea or at a shift between ideas. If you are utilizing slides, make certain that what is shown accompanies what you are stating.

Gestures are motions of the arms, hands, shoulders and head to assist you in communicating. They play an essential role in public speaking, yet they need to boost communication and not impede it. Attempt making the gestures when rehearsing. Practice in front of a mirror, even to the point of overemphasizing. Then adjust your gestures to a point where they are natural and appropriate. Nevertheless, gestures ought to be spontaneous. Using too many gestures might sidetrack the audience.

One sort of gesture is the facial expression. This demonstrates your mindsets and sensations. Let your face burn with enthusiasm or radiate with happiness. Stay away from wearing the deadpan poker face which reveals absolutely nothing. This does not imply that you are going to constantly give vent to your feelings in an overblown and lavish way. A great speaker expresses views with proper restraint.

Eye contact is a really essential factor in getting and maintaining attention. Take a look at your listeners straight, not above them or at the floor or ceiling or out of the window; otherwise, you lose your contact with your audience, and their attention strays off.

Here are certains questions you may think about so as to assist your visual delivery:

- Do I gesture sufficiently?

- Does my body language strengthen the speech flow?

- Are my gestures irritating anyhow?

- Do I depend a lot on any one gesture?

- Does my face express the significance or sensation I am attempting to communicate?

- Are there various gestures, body motions, or facial expressions which may show my designated meaning better?

Vocal Delivery

All of us enjoy having an effective voice. Voice is important in communication; just through it can any speech delivery be achieved.

An excellent voice is natural, conversational, and passionate. It is enjoyable to hear without even aiming to be. The audience is going to listen more if you speak as you do in a regular conversation.

Sounds have 4 essential attributes: volume, rate, pitch, and quality. If either of these is faulty, distraction happens. Essential statements are said in a slow way and with a fairly low pitch, whereas light remarks or jokes are said in a quick fashion with a reasonably higher pitch.

1. Volume.

A properly-modulated voice is essential to be a successful speaker. Plenty of individuals have extremely soft voices, which could be because of shyness or absence of training or absence of practice in voice projection. Individuals with soft voices are typically regarded as dull. An individual who wishes to establish an appealing, pleasing, and vibrant personality must go through training in voice projection.

There is no set rule about the degree of volume that ought to be utilized on various occasions, however, an effective voice needs to be as loud as the particular speaking circumstance requires. If you are speaking with a group, each member of the audience with typical concentration and hearing ought to have the ability to comprehend your declarations without straining their ears and without getting aggravated due to an exceedingly loud voice. Great speakers fit actions and voice to the words utilized, to the circumstance, and to their personalities. A crucial principle in speaking plainly is that consonants ought to be pronounced properly. Vowels are simpler to pronounce, yet consonants provide intelligibility to speech.

A voice which is controlled by intelligence instead of emotion has a tendency to be moderate in pitch and also in volume. This does not indicate that intellectual efforts are without feeling. It simply indicates that intellectual efforts accompanied by vocalization are not generally defined by the overstated intensity and range of feelings displayed in emotional habits alone.

2. Pitch.

Pitch is the overall level on a musical scale of the voice in speech. If an individual is repeatedly tense, the voice is typically at a higher pitch level than that of a repeatedly unwinded individual. Pitch might either be low, medium or high; or we might utilize terms such as alto, soprano, baritone, or bass for vocal pitch.

Natural speaking pitch is essential for an effective voice. One who unnaturally speaks is going to be disagreeable, ineffective, and uneasy.

3. Rate.

There are 3 rates or pace in speaking-- slow, ordinary, and quick. A noticeably slow speaking rate shows solemnity, sadness, or depression. A significant boost in rate is suggestive of joy, happiness, elation, or anger. Words or expressions which are spoken more gradually and more emphatically are considered more vital and more intellectually substantial than quickly pronounced words. Nevertheless, a continual, unvarying rate of speaking is dissuaded regardless of feeling, state of mind, or objective since it is dull.

Modifications in rate could be accomplished by the use of pauses or by the rate of articulation. Making use of pauses is a really beneficial method for separating or assembling phrases, for developing significant impacts, and for stressing ideas. As a basic guideline, making use of a comma is an indication for the speaker or reader to pause. However, in certain circumstances, long sentences without commas ought to additionally be divided according to thought content by a pause to offer time for breathing and for the listener to comprehend totally what is being said or read.

The dramatic impact could be accomplished by speakers who pause after an increasing inflection, therefore developing suspense; after which the anticipated result follows to the fulfillment of their listeners. Successful speakers, nevertheless, ought to stay away from pauses showing that they do not understand what to say next. Speakers who understand how to pause without fear and with intent are respected speakers.

4. Quality.

Voice attributes (or voice timbre) and voice attitudes (or voice color) come under the basic term of voice quality. An individual's voice could be classified as unpleasant or pleasant, based upon its timbre and color or quality. What is voice quality? This term is tough to pinpoint, and no effort is going to be made to specify it here other than to show its relation to other elements and how to attain this. Singing quality is connected to resonance and to the avoidance of unfavorable vocal elements like extreme nasality and breathing. It is additionally associated with feelings and state of mind.

Verbal Delivery.

Besides being significantly conscious of vocal delivery (manner of speaking) and your visual delivery (you and your visual aids), the audience is going to concentrate on your verbal delivery (the language you utilize and how you build sentences). Listeners like speakers who utilize a more casual language than what is ordinary for written reports. For example, in oral speech, it is better suited to utilize brief, easy sentences, and it is not constantly needed to utilize total sentences. Furthermore, it is definitely appropriate to utilize individual pronouns like I, we, you, and us and contractions like I'm and don't-- forms which are regularly avoided in formal written reports.

One misstep is to utilize long or exceptionally technical terms or lingo to impress the audience. Despite the fact that you are speaking in an expert setting, do not believe that your listeners utilize or comprehend the identical technical words or lingo that you do. The ideal language is lively and vibrant (paints a picture for the audience), concrete and particular (provides details), and straightforward.

Placing your ideas into easy-to-comprehend language which fits the contexts of your audience and is vibrant, particular, and bias-free could be challenging at the start. As you practice on the fundamentals of delivery, nevertheless, keep in mind the guidelines gone over here, and your style of speaking and language are going to advance.

Approaches of Delivery

There are 4 techniques for delivering a speech: manuscript reading, impromptu, extemporaneous and memorization.

1. The Impromptu Speech

Of the 4 techniques, impromptu speech needs the least prep. With really little notice in advance, the speaker is asked to speak for a couple of minutes on a particular topic.

Attempt to use the following guidelines or rules in delivering an impromptu speech.

1. Develop the main idea. Do not attempt to go over the whole topic. Restrict yourself to a particular element which you could talk about in a couple of minutes. Make sure you understand the idea you wish to present before you begin.

2. Open your talk with a sentence which states something. Do not be supplicating. Start with a bang, and go directly to the point.

3. Your speech's body needs to be merged. You could provide instances, illustrations, contrasts, and

comparisons to assist in describing your crucial sentences. Be as concrete and particular as feasible.

4. End on a powerful note. You could repeat your crucial sentences while rephrasing them. Reiterate them quickly but plainly.

Here are other standards when it comes to delivering an impromptu speech:

- Anticipate the possibility that you may be called on to speak, so make certain preparations early.

- Make the most of whichever tiny amount of preparation time you are provided with.

- Practice active listening.

- Handle speech anxiety by reminding yourself that nobody expects you to be flawless when you have to deliver impromptu speeches.

- Utilize the basic guidelines of speech organization.

- Think about the impromptu speech as delivering a golden chance to practice and establish your delivery.

2. The Manuscript Speech

A manuscript or read speech is one which is drawn up and read word for word throughout delivery. When the event is a historical or solemn one, the read speech is the most proper. Individuals of prominence read their speeches for precision and accuracy. This sort of speech does not have naturalness and spontaneity which the extemporaneous speech or the impromptu speech has. The speaker must preserve rapport with the audience.

Here are certain rules for providing a manuscript speech:

- Utilize a manuscript for the appropriate explanations.

- Utilize an excellent oral style.

- Practice intensively.

- Try to find chances to gesture and move.

- Utilize your voice successfully.

- Stay flexible.

3. The Memorized Speech

This technique of delivery is excellent just for elocution pieces. Like the read speech, it does not have naturalness and spontaneity. Additionally, human memory may fail the speaker throughout the delivery and could cause excellent humiliation. This kind of speech must not be utilized in public speaking classes.

Here are certain guidelines in delivering a memorized speech:

- Remain concentrated on your particular objective and on the vital ideas you wish to communicate.

- Speak at the moment.

- Practice, practice, practice!

4. The Extemporaneous Speech

This technique is advised for public speaking classes. It is not memorized nor read. It has naturalness and spontaneity. The speaker additionally has time to prepare the ideas embodied in it, though the language is developed at the moment of delivery. This speech is additionally practiced, yet the words and setup of words are altered to something much better and more helpful. In rehearsing, the speaker is just directed by a psychological outline. If notes are held, these just include quotes from popular speakers and authors which assist in expounding the ideas. The speaker does not memorize the speech; however, he understands from memory the order of ideas to attain organization, unity, and clarity in speech.

An extemporaneous speech:

- Requires cautious preparation.

- Is based upon a key word outline.

- Enables the speaker to stay involved, direct, and versatile.

Practicing Your Speech

Sometimes, the majority of speakers go through the outline calmly a couple of times and believe they are ready for delivery. Absolutely nothing could be further from reality. If you have actually not practiced your speech aloud numerous times, more than likely, you are not ready to speak. There is an excellent distinction between reading about how to hold a successful speech and really doing it. The only way to transform what you have actually read into what you could do is to practice it. Remember that your goal is to be natural and sound confident, much like speaking with buddies. If you have actually been visualizing yourself delivering an effective speech, you have actually taken an important initial move towards confident delivery. Great or bad speeches are a matter of habit. Habits are created and established with consistent practice.

Feeling great while speaking is among the benefits of practicing. The ideal results are attained if you prepare in 2 ways:

1. By visualizing yourself delivering a successful and effective speech, and,

2. By, in fact, practicing your speech aloud.

Here are the guidelines when practicing your speech.

- First, go through your speech quietly numerous times up until you are prepared to start. Nevertheless, doing this is not practicing speech delivery. It might assist you to look for issues of organization and might assist you in acquainting yourself with the material, however, it will not assist in any way with your visual and vocal delivery and is going to just assist a bit with your verbal delivery.

- Practice delivering your speech aloud with your outline and notes. There is no substitute for practicing aloud, standing on your feet, utilizing your visual aids and notes, practicing your eye contact and gestures, and speaking aloud.

- Stand straight, if you can, in front of a full-length mirror put at a distance where your audience would be.

- For the initial rehearsals, utilize your outline up until you are certain of your primary points and their order.

- After the initial practice session, pause and ask yourself if the order you followed is the ideal order of ideas feasible, if the material you collected suffices, if the way you expressed your ideas is the most effective, and if your selection of words is suitable.

- Practice your speech aloud -- keeping in mind rough parts, rereading your notes, and after that practicing again.

- Split the speech into parts and practice significant parts, like the introduction, a number of times continuously.

- Repeat the session as many times as required up until you have gotten self-assurance and self-confidence, taking note of the correct pronunciation and enunciation of your consonants and vowels, suitable phrasing and pausing, stress, optimal volume and pitch.

- When you are fairly certain of your significant subtopics and headings and their order, you might place aside your outline and practice with just your notes. (Notes here imply saying quotations from well-known speakers and authors that you wish to quote to drive home a point.).

- Constantly take breaks. Stay away from practicing so much at once that you start to lose your voice, energy, or focus.

- Practice on your own initially. Record (either video or audio) your speech and play it back so as to obtain feedback on your vocal delivery. Stay away from dissecting your delivery. Focus on significant issues.

- If feasible, go to the room where you are going to practice and speak utilizing the equipment there or practice in a room comparable to the one in which you are going to be speaking. If your practice room does not have the tools required for utilizing your visuals, mimic handling them. If you are delivering a manuscript speech, ensure that the manuscript is double- or triple-spaced in 14 or 16-point type. Put manuscript pages into a stiff binder. Practice holding the binder high enough that you are able to look down at the manuscript without needing to bob your head.

- When you start to feel comfy with your speech, practice before a little audience (buddies or members of the family). Ask them for particular remarks and feedback on your visual, verbal, and vocal delivery. Practice utilizing gestures and making direct eye contact. If you have a camera, let a buddy record you to ensure that you could observe yourself. If you find any uncomfortable spots in your speech, choose how to customize the speech to smooth them out.

- Over an amount of time, practice your speech numerous times, completely, however, guard versus memorization. Keep in mind that practice does not mean just to memorize.

- Make certain to time yourself numerous times. If your speech is too long, make proper cuts. For instance, you may cut a part that is less important, utilize less illustrations, modify long quotes, or plan to tell the audience that you are going to be glad to resolve a problem more completely throughout the question-and-answer duration. Keep in mind that, if your speech is too long or too brief, you might break the audience's expectations and harm your trustworthiness.

- At least one time prior to the actual speech (2 or 3 times would be better), practice utilizing your visual aids with all the required tools. Video yourself, if you can, or ask a buddy to observe one of your last practices.

- Attempt to get sufficient sleep the night prior to your speech. On the day of the speech, get to the location early to ensure that you are able to compose yourself. See that your visuals and notes remain in the correct order, and go through your outline one final time.

Keep in mind that nobody expects you to be flawless. If you make an error, remedy it if required and continue. Then forget it. If you have actually practiced until you feel comfy with your speech and have actually imagined yourself delivering a good speech, you ought to feel passionate and confident.

Reaction to Audience Questions

The secret to effective question-and-answer durations is really to understand your subject and expect questions from the audience. Among the most discouraging aspects of speaking is needing to remove so much crucial information (both private and research-based) from your speech due to time restraints. However, if you are preparing a question-and-answer duration to go with your speech, it is practically inconceivable to understand all the things about your subject. The more you understand, the better your responses are going to be.

Aside from understanding your subject, expect numerous questions that you believe your audience might ask and prepare a couple of visual aids to utilize when responding to these questions. Prior to preparing completely brand-new visuals, see if one or more overlays (for example, one with a line chart which contains brand-new information) might be featured in a visual that you wish to utilize in your speech. The overlays would be utilized just throughout the question-and-answer duration. Definitely, it's possible that none of these questions are going to be asked. However, just in case, you could impress your audience significantly.

The following ideas might assist you with your question-and-answer duration. If you do a good job with audience questions, you could make your message more persuading.

- Listen diligently to every question asked.

- If suitable, repeat the question prior to addressing it so that everybody could hear it and track what is happening.

- Rephrase any complicated or negative questions in a clear and good way.

- Think a moment prior to responding to every question. If you do not know the response, say so, and refer the questioner to somebody in the audience who does know. Or, tell the individual that it's a great question to which you are going to discover the response to and let that individual know at the following conference.

- Do not let someone control the forum duration.

- If you believe a question is unimportant or is going to take too long to address, thank the individual for the question and point out that you are going to speak with that person personally about it after the duration.

- Do not attempt to fake your way through an answer.

- Do not argue or become defensive or angry while addressing questions. What you say throughout the question-and-answer duration is going to affect the audience's general judgment of your reliability and your speech.

- If suitable, actively urge listeners to get involved.

- If you anticipate a hostile audience, stay away from a question-and-answer duration in any way you can. If not, point out in your introduction that there is going to be a brief question-and-answer duration at the end of your speech and ask the audience to draw up questions throughout the speech. After your preliminary conclusion, gather the questions, choose 3 or 4 good ones, and address them--disregarding the less pleasing ones.

- Monitor your time and end the duration with the last conclusion which refocuses the audience's attention and places a pleasant closure on your speech.

Public Speaking Fear

Learn How to Beat the Fear of Public Speaking so That You Can Be Confident and Deliver the Speech Which Will Inspire Your Audience

By Clark Darsey

Introduction to Public Speaking Fear

All human relationships are built upon effective language in speaking. Doors and opportunities open for people who know their way with words and who can speak well. Oral presentations are similar to any other human interaction with the scale being much, much larger. These kinds of events also have an effect on the relationships on a more intimate level.

A lot of people have a lot of anxiety when they only think of speaking in public. There is really no need for that and you can combat this easily. This kind of performance has been a part of our history for many centuries and it is held in pretty high regard by many.

Some people are excited by the possible challenge offered by public speaking while others don't even want to hear or think about having to give a speech. A lot of people have a lot of interest in getting over the fear of public speaking. Public speaking is among the most frightening things most people don't want to go through. The fear of public speaking takes the top spot, followed by a fear of death.

Even though speaking in front of an audience may be overwhelming, it is possible for a lot of people to overcome this fear. It is necessary to understand public speaking in order to be successful in overcoming this fear.

This book is all about describing public speaking so that you could understand and control your fears to a greater extent. After reading this book, you will be equipped with strategies that will make it more than possible for you to deliver a quality speech no matter if a speech is over video or on a stage during a special occasion.

Chapter 1: About Public Speaking

Public speaking refers to any talking that is done in front of a group of individuals. The size of the group doesn't really change the definition of public speaking. Whatever the case may be, this whole process is quite an ordeal for most folks.

Public speaking is an art form. There are no good speeches without crisp delivery that consist of pauses which emphasize what is important. Some people seem to be natural at this kind of performances while others can never seem to have their way with public speaking.

It is helpful if someone is naturally talented. Regardless, a person can become good at public speaking by being patient and practicing diligently. Knowing how to give an oral presentation can be learned if one knows what to do without getting discouraged. In order for a public speaking performance to be effective, it is necessary to have a certain structure and a purpose. Having a plan instead of winging it is what can make up for the lack of inherent talent and it is what separates pros from the amateurs.

There are a lot of reasons for public speaking occasions. Public speaking can be entertaining, for better or worse. Public speaking can also be informative and educational and it can have an influence on other people. It is necessary to have the purpose of the speech in mind in order to achieve a greater level of organization of thoughts and information.

Key Elements of Public Speaking

People can be very different based on the occasion and the context. People adapt to their environment. Before speaking in public, there are some things that need to be considered in order for the presentation to go well.

The first element of speaking in public is the individual who is delivering a particular speech. This person who is delivering a speech really has to think about how the speech will be perceived by the audience. What is really neat about public speaking is the fact that the speech can be personalized based on someone's presentation style.

The key element of public speaking is the message which is attempted to be conveyed. It is necessary to know clearly what kind of information is attempted to be presented. Good information is very important for any public speaking performance. A presentation which is well organized can make or break the whole event.

Another key element of public speaking is the method. The method can encompass many things such as the location where the speech will be held, prompts that would be used and so on.

The last element of public speaking is the reason why the speech is held in the first place. It is necessary to know whether the speech is of the informative kind or is it leaning more towards the entertainment side. Another possibility is in public speaking having the goal of influencing and motivating people.

Public Speaking Over the Years

Signs and traces of public speaking can be found in any civilization through history if one looks hard enough. There has always been a lot of value in the spoken word ever since people were around. Being able to communicate in this way is what has enabled humans to make as much progress as they have.

Communicating orally was the at the forefront until written communication saw the light of day. Thanks to the written communication, many valuable works were preserved so that future generations could benefit from them and find enjoyment in them.

Poetry was created as a necessity in order to make memorization that much easier. Stories and words would be much easier to commit to memory if they rhymed and this made it a lot easier for those who would go through with oral presentations.

Many civilizations over the history place importance upon the spoken word. No sphere of life could be separated from debating a discussing. Politics and religion are simply a byproduct of this.

Public Speaking in Today's World

Public speaking is very prevalent in a lot of aspects of our lives today. We are continuously informed and influenced by oral presentations. Spoken word is the main way of dealing with family and other people with whom we may want to connect with. It is possible to communicate with people on a global scale thanks to the massive advancements in the technology. Before, it would take a lot longer for word to reach its intended destination. Most messages can get from one end of the globe to the other instantly with the aid of the technology.

There are a lot of ways to go along with public speaking today and one example of this would be videoconferences. This way, the presenter can deliver a speech to many people without even coming in contact with the audience. It was never easier to communicate with the masses thanks to the rise of the communication technology.

Opportunities and Events

Telecommunications is what allows you to deliver your message although some people may find it weird speaking to something that doesn't provide them with any sort of feedback. Of course, there will always be opportunities where quality oral presentations will have to be delivered to a group of people right on the spot.

All events are different and some event may be of the informative nature. For example, it may be necessary to deliver a speech with the objective of warning people about the possible hazards in the workplace. If the speech is a good one, then a lot of people could be moved in a way which benefits you.

Some events could also be of the personal kind. For example, your friend may be getting married and the pressure could be placed upon you to deliver a great speech. It is necessary to be prepared in order for the message to get across successfully to the recipients, whoever they may be.

Chapter 2: Fears and Phobias

Merely thinking about delivering a speech in front of a group of people can overwhelm a person, but it is necessary to slow down and to remember the difference between fears and phobias. Things may be a bit more complicated than you simply being afraid of the task at hand. A phobia may be in question and if that is the case, then there are certain precautions that need to be taken care of.

Fear can be pretty heavy and overpowering, but it is necessary to be able to differentiate between the fear and the phobia. There are differences and similarities between the two and it is necessary to understand them in order to get to the best possible conclusion. If a phobia is in question, then a professional may need to be consulted.

About Fear

Fear is an emotion which is important and it does play a pretty crucial role. Fear exists in order to ensure that people stay out of trouble so that their chances of surviving would increase. It is all about self-preservation. Without fear, people would be doing dangerous things without a second thought. Survival of all people would be in question if fear didn't exist and fear is, therefore, good and we should be glad we have it.

Even though the explanation may be simple, fear is a bit more complicated and there are layers to it. Fear is a part of every human in order to ensure that they remain safe. Of course, people are different, and not everyone will feel the fear and anxiety to the same extent.

The body does react to the emotion of fear quite prominently. When people feel fear, they will feel the physical changes in their bodies. What truly happens is that autonomic nervous system gets fired up along with the activation of adrenal glands. People are very aware of the feeling of fear and how it feels physically. Most frequent symptoms are shaking, being tense and breathing rapidly. There is also a chance of faster heart rate, sweat and dry mouth as a result of fear. Blood is redirected from the brain towards other body parts which may have a greater need for the energy in order to tackle the challenge at hand.

This redirection of the blood flow from the brain towards the other parts of the body can be quite quick and some lightheadedness and dizziness could be experienced by some people as a consequence. The situations that make people fearful also tend to activate the fight or flight mechanism which mobilizes the person to either run away or to stand ground.

Only fears people are born with are the fear of falling and fear of loud noises. Any other fear is learned in some way. It is still unclear in the scientific community how helpful fear is as far as protecting people and to what extent are fears learnable. What is certain is the fact that the enviroment plays a role in the formation of fear.

About Phobias

Phobias are fears that are very specific and that are unreasonable in their magnitude to the point of being irrational. Phobias can easily be distinguished from regular fear by realizing that phobias are irrational and unreasonable given the circumstances. Phobias are actually a lot more common than you may think.

In some cases, phobias can be on the level of psychological disorders if it negatively impacts the ability of the person to go along with their everyday life in a satisfactory manner. For example, a phobia of dogs may not by itself warrant classification as a psychological disorder. However, such a phobia that would prevent a person from going into households that have a pet dog could be classified as a disorder.

Categories of Phobias

There are three categories of phobias which are recognized. The first category are simple phobias and those phobias are fears of things and situations which aren't rational. The second category of phobias are social phobias and those are unreasonable fears of social settings and occasions. The last category of phobias is agoraphobia which is the fear of not being able to get out of a certain situation.

Simple phobias can vary quite a bit and they can extend to all kinds of things and situations. Someone with this phobia wants to get away from certain things and situations as much as possible. The person with this phobia actually realizes the irrationality of it all and that is why those people don't necessarily always look for a treatment for their phobia.

Social phobias tend to be paralyzing to anyone who happens to suffer from them. Obviously, just thinking about public speaking would terrify a person dealing with this. The fear of public scrutiny would be way too paralyzing for someone suffering from this kind of phobia.

At first, agoraphobia was just considered to be a fear of wide open spaces. However, recent findings have indicated that the people who may be dealing with this don't want to leave the safety of their homes because they are afraid of finding themselves in a situation they can't get out of. Panic attacks are what can influence the development of agoraphobia since people don't want for those panic attacks to happen in an inconvenient situation.

All of these phobias are viewed as anxiety disorders. Possible treatment options for these conditions are cognitive behavioral therapy or medication. A combination of these two is also an option. Any other treatment option is likely a variant of cognitive behavioral therapy, such as gradual exposure to unpleasantness with the goal of desensitization.

Glossophobia

There are some important differences between phobias and fears. Fears are an essential part of our survival and self-preservation. As long as fears don't get out of control, they shouldn't interfere with the regular conduct of everyday life. On the other hand, phobias are over the top, irrational and excessive. There is a lot of anxiety when merely thinking about a situation which is the source of phobia. Phobia can impair an individual, unlike fear.

People that are afraid of public speaking may not be delighted with the fact that they have to go through with public speaking, but they can still do it even though they may not do everything perfectly. Such a person could lose their train of thought during a speech, but they would still manage to wrap it up successfully. There is nothing stopping this individual from going through with the public speaking performance.

However, someone who is dealing with glossophobia may not be able to do as well in a similar situation. Just thinking about public speaking would be enough for the paralyzing anxiety to ensue. To make things even worse, physical symptoms may also be present, such as nausea. People dealing with glossophobia avoid situations where they would have to address an audience like a plague.

There are physical reactions to glossophobia and those aren't too dissimilar from the fight or flight reaction. Fight or flight response consists of faster heart rate, a spike in blood pressure, rigidity in the muscles etc. Senses would also be heightened since the individual is expecting trouble, even though they don't feel like they could handle it due to the general feeling of lightheadedness. Fainting is also a possibility.

Certain people will try to speak in public and they will start exhibiting signs of speaking disorders which they never knew they had. They may also start to stutter and a bit more challenging words will tend to be difficult to articulate fluently. What used to be simple is hard, all of sudden.

Glossophobia is specific to public speaking. Some people may be suffering from this, but they may be able to mask it such as in situations like dancing and singing. One way to get over the anxiety of giving speeches is for the person to imagines themselves as an actor since that puts ideas of proactivity in someone's mind.

Chapter 3: Roots of Public Speaking Fear

The best way to get over a certain fear is to realize what is the root cause behind all of it. Fear is a crucial self-preserving emotion that protects us for the most part. It is one of those emotions that are a part of human DNA with the purpose of keeping us out of trouble. The fear of public speaking is rooted in self-preservation as well.

Fears are learnable since the only fears we are born with are the fear of falling and fear of loud noises. A certain fear can form based on someone's experiences. Interestingly enough, some people can develop fears by just seeing other people being afraid of something.

Everyone knows logically that there is no real threat during speaking in public. Still, some of the self-preserving emotions tend to get activated in these kinds of situations. Fear of public speaking isn't so simple since it combines our hardwired instincts with the fears which have been learned experientially.

Instinctual Fears

Public speaking is an overwhelming social scenario and there is a natural response to it. This reaction may actually have a purpose and it may be more than a mere annoyance. This reaction can be a form of self-preservation.

There are certain instinctual fears which are hardwired into humans. The purpose of these fears is to aid us so that we could make quality decisions under pressure so that we would stay out of trouble. Fear is a natural reaction even though it may not be pleasant for the body and the mind.

Fear is a form of a message which conveys that there is danger around. People are hardwired to be afraid of anything that can point to danger. High places are one example of something people are supposed to be afraid of. Our bodily reactions have to be strong so that we would realize that it is necessary to take action promptly.

Fear of public speaking is deeply ingrained in the human psyche and it seems that public speaking itself provides perfect conditions for this to be the case. It really shouldn't be surprising that the reaction to public speaking is such as it is since facing a whole crowd of people head-on isn't the most peaceful predicament to be in.

It is easy to get the fight or flight response activated if someone isn't prepared properly. A speaker probably knows on a logical level that the audience means no harm, but there still may be unease and an urge to seek some kind of protection. This is what makes this particular fear of public speaking universal to all people to some point.

Fears Which are Learned

A lot of fears can be learned through experience. Someone can learn to fear certain things and/or scenarios based on past experiences. A small child may not fear dogs at first until a certain experience teaches him otherwise. There are a lot of different experiences that can aid in the formation of fear.

Let's take dogs as an example, a child may learn to be afraid of motorcycles simply by observing someone else being visibly afraid of dogs. A child can also learn to fear dogs if an accident of some kind is witnessed from a distance, such as a dog bite.

Don't underestimate the power of the mind since it can have a large effect on most fears. Just imagining the experiences which tend to make someone fearful can be all that is necessary since a mind won't be able to tell the difference between the imagination and the real thing if the imagination is vivid enough.

How Does the Fear of Public Speaking Develop

There are not many people who will not be somewhat intimidated when they are faced with the task of public speaking. The fear of public speaking has its fair share of inherent fears. Some fears can be completely imaginary while others may be subtle and not so obvious. Everyone will have their own reasons why they feel anxiety about public speaking.

It is possible that some people may have had a traumatic experience when it comes to public speaking. Events such as these can have implications that can last a while. Only one bad experience related to public speaking can be all that it takes in order for someone to become afraid of speaking in front of groups of people.

A momentary fear that is intense enough can impact someone's whole life. Our nervous system simply works by associating fear with situations which could be bad and which should be avoided. The body will respond accordingly if anxiety and dread are felt during an event.

People naturally associate how they feel with what happened. Some people get the fear ingrained in them faster than others. Sometimes negative associations may not be connected with the act of public speaking in the slightest since a negative association could be formed just in someone's mind.

Most people learn to fear public speaking because of associations. It may be enough to be the witness of someone else's bad experience with public speaking in order for the bad associations to be formed. If the instance of public speaking is bad enough, then the observer will be weary of similar situations as well. A similar example would be a child learning to fear dogs because of witnessing someone else entirely getting bitten. Fear can be formed by just seeing the traumatizing event.

How Fear Builds Over Time

Fear of public speaking can also be developed over time little by little. An instance of stage fright which is very minor can evolve into something more serious if this accumulation is left unattended and ignored. The fear only grows stronger if someone focuses on it directly.

Very subtle experiences can compound into a fear which turns out to be overwhelming. The body overreacts since the response to the emotion of fear is too much alluring. If a mind belives something, then the body will do so as well and the feeling of anxiety can activate the nervous system.

The way in which fear compounds upon itself gradually can be explained by Pavlov's behavioral experiments. It is well known that Pavlov's dogs respond inappropriately to the bells being rung. It is actually a quite simple experiment. Just as dogs were about to be fed, the bells would be rung. It didn't take long for the dogs to start salivating when they merely hear the sound regardless if the food is served or not. The way their body would respond became tied with the sound of the bell.

There is a lot of power in associations. A mind can always make the experience seem worse than it actually is. Never forget that you are, for the most part, in the control of what you think and how you feel. You can rewire your body so that it responds differently to public speaking events and occasions.

Chapter 4: How Can You Unlearn Your Fears

Just as the associations to certain stimuli can be created, they can be unlearned as well if someone knows what to do. It is necessary to have the patience for this to be a success, but it is worth the effort. There are several ways in which reactions to things and situations can be relearned and rewired.

One way to unlearn your fears of public speaking is to adopt a cognitive approach. By doing this, you are deliberately using logic and rationality by constantly reminding yourself that the fear is not based in reality. It does require time to get used to working with emotions, but it is very possible to successfully adopt the cognitive approach by doing so.

A behavioral approach can also be utilized in order to change how you respond. Experts on behavioral psychology tend to refer to this approach as operant conditioning. Just as bad experiences can be anxiety provoking, the positive experiences can, in the same way, create pleasant feelings.

What you have to do is to keep reminding yourself that the fear of public speaking isn't based in reality and that there aren't any threats to your safety you should be worried about. Still, this kind of fear is pretty universal to people. The same feeling of fear and anxiety can be turned around into feelings of excitement and thrill.

You Can Unlearn the Fears You Have Learned

People use their set of beliefs as a guide through life. Some of those beliefs are factual while others are merely a product of faith. Some beliefs may be based on the perspective which is simply wrong.

Fear of public speaking is mostly rooted in a perspective that isn't based in reality and which doesn't make sense. Even though you may be anxious about public speaking, there may not be anything that would serve as a plausible explanation for those feelings. Most people who learn the fear of public speaking in front of crowds do so because of certain experiences and perceptions.

People stumble because of the way in which they perceive their audience. The audience isn't really a threat, but the person afraid of public speaking thinks otherwise. The nervous system is primed to respond to a certain fear if the mind and body come to the conclusion that there is a certain danger that justifies the reaction.

Only one traumatic event can cascade into phobias and fears for a lifetime even if the event itself was very brief. Just witnessing the event could be all that it takes. The good news is that someone can learn to be fearless again with some practice. Several positive events can be what is necessary to undo the damage of one bad event.

How to Gain Control

It is well known in a field of cognitive therapy that someone who takes a cognitive approach when dealing with a certain situation, makes an attempt to resolve an issue with a deliberate thought. In order to do this successfully, it is necessary to distance yourself from the emotions itself and this can be very fruitful even though it is not easy.

It is not easy to be objective and this is especially true when emotions are involved in the equation. Practice is required in order for the cognitive approach to work, but you can regain control of how you look at public speaking occasions.

What you think and what you feel is connected pretty tightly. You ultimately have control of what you think and you can use what you think to take control of what you feel. In order to rise above the anxiety and fear of public speaking, it is necessary to always be reminding yourself of certain facts about public speaking. There are no inherent dangers to public speaking. Your presentation doesn't have to be completely perfect. Everyone makes mistakes and they are a part of life. Whichever outcomes you are fearing are not realistic. The audience is not against you and it isn't out there to get you. You can't possibly control everything about the presentation.

Everyone will need to approach their fears differently since all people are different. A presentation contains different components and they all contain certain elements of fear for different people. You have to really think about which aspect of public speaking has the most effect on you so that you can cater your thoughts accordingly.

How to Change Your Response

Thoughts can be retrained and emotional responses to certain things and circumstances can also be changed. Desensitization is how reactions to fear can be minimized and this is at the core of exposure therapy which is all about gradually exposing a person to what that person is afraid of.

It is possible to get rid of the fear and a success rate is pretty high among people who commit to using strategies like desensitization and exposure therapy. In order to increase the chances of success and to save time, it is recommended to utilize these strategies intensively in a shorter period of time instead of doing the same thing over longer periods of time with lower intensity. It is necessary to be careful and to know how much intensity is enough in order to not make the fear even worse.

How Can You Desensetize Yourself to Fear

Esentially, desensitization and exposure therapy can be used by people to get over their fears. One way of doing this is to replace bad memories with positive ones. This can actually be quite simple and there is no need to overcomplicate things.

The memories of a certain fear reside within the region of the brain called the amygdala. When someone tries to control the emotion, that process starts in the region of the brain which is called medial prefrontal cortex which is the rational part of the brain and which sends signals to the amygdala and to the brain stem. Just like the fear response can be based in the amygdala, the feeling that a certain situation is safe can also be based within the amygdala.

People should be placed within the reach of new experiences that share the same source of fear with the thing they are persistently afraid of. It is possible to retrain the brain so that a person could relearn how to react to something in a more healthy manner. It is quite possible to instill the feeling of safety within the amygdala. When this is done successfully, the brain stem, which is a part of the brain responsible for automatic behavior such as beating of the heart and breathing, is also affected in a positive way since a person will be less likely to physically overreact by starting to breathe more shallowly, for example.

This is all possible by making sure that the slow and gradual exposure to the source of fear is accompanied by positive experiences so that positive associations would be formed. In the same way, people who are afraid of public speaking can get themselves exposed to very small doses of public speaking at first while also deriving some pleasure from the experience. If the experience turns out to be a pleasurable one, then this pleasantness is communicated by the medial prefrontal cortex to the brain stem and the amygdala. Bad memories in the brain can be replaced with more positive ones and this is how the reactions to fear responses are controlled.

There are people who swear that this whole process doesn't take more than a couple of hours while some other people suggest that a lot more time of someone exposing themselves to public speaking is necessary. At the end of the day, it all depends upon the individual.

Chapter 5: The Importance of the Audience

You should never underestimate the importance of audience in public speaking occasions. It is important to have a healthy understanding of the audience in order for the presentation to be a success. This can allow you to have a greater level of control over the crowd and to start establishing rapport if you manage to be empathetic enough.

This may seem overwhelming, but you should quickly come to the conclusion that the audience is your ally and that you should treat it so. A successful presentation can't be one sided. Using the visualization to portray the audience as an ally can provide someone with great public speaking success.

No matter which flaws someone may have with public speaking, they can be turned around and a person can become a public speaking star. It is all about knowing how to perform well in order to overcome the possible issues with articulation.

If you are sufficiently inspired, you can gain control over the situation in order to get the most out of the approach that would provide you, as an individual, with the best results. You can achieve what you set your mind to, whether that is to create a personality around your public speaking or to build rapport with your audience.

Your Audience Wants to Help You Succeed

Most of the anxiety that comes with public speaking can be traced to the faulty perception of the audience. If the audience is seen as the threat and as the enemy, then it can be very easy for the fear to develop. You will do a lot more good for your success if you reframe this and start thinking that the audience wants to see you succeed with the presentation.

Empathy is very important. Any member of your audience is likely to be weary of public speaking just like you are. The audience may be acutely aware of what you are going through and this can provide a presenter with a sense of calmness.

It is a fact that people like to see the demonstration of confidence. However, adding in some humor and humility can lift the presentation to a whole new level. Public speaking is an interactive kind of event. You should always keep in mind that the audience can overlook if you are not completely perfect with your public speaking, just like someone in a one on one conversation won't mind that much if you mess up a sentence.

You may think that a certain slip of the tongue or a stutter is a deal breaker, but it means barely anything to the people in the audience. It is the fact that you are your harshest critic and that you judge yourself way more than other people do. No one will criticize your presentation as much as you will.

Manage Your Expectations

It is not easy to manage your expectations as far as the audience is concerned. A person who happens to enjoy speaking in public may enjoy the task of public speaking itself since he or she understanding the importance of meeting the expectation of the audience.

When you are seeing a movie, the lines are delivered perfectly since they are rehearsed and practiced. The lines are rehearsed with the knowledge of what it is being expected and this is what makes it possible to deliver the line properly. Some people may be overwhelmed when they merely think of the expectations of the audience. Still, you can use these same expectations to get over your fear.

You can draw inspiration from the expectations of your audience. You should be aware of the purpose of your speech and about the information that your audience is expecting to get out of the whole occassion so that you could organize things properly. By being empathetic, you can assume the position of the audience in order to realize what are they expecting you to deliver on. You could also develop an understanding of whether you, as an audience member, would mind if the speaker made a slight mistake.

Motivation

Fear of public speaking can prevent a lot of people from going after what they want. You don't necessarily have to be very outgoing to be good at public speaking since there are many shy people who can do well with public speaking. Nature of the public speaking performance can be used to get over issues such as stuttering.

Some people may have a stuttering issue which is also preventing them from doing well in numerous social situations. There are ways in which this can be overcome by reading books aloud and working on the enunciation and articulation. This is a very simple approach, but doing it over the course of time can yield very impressive results in the public speaking department, even if a lot of people say that a certain individual would never amount to much in terms of public speaking. Such people actually tend to make the largest splash.

Don't Worry About the Control So Much

It is possible to rise above the challenges as long you really put your mind to getting better at public speaking. Some people worry about control and that is a huge hurdle for them. The act of public speaking is interactive, for the most part, but it is necessary to stop worrying about control so much in order to rise above the fear.

What you feel, other people feel as well. If you are feeling anxious, then you can be certain that other people will feel that. It may happen that some members of the audience are fidgeting which pretty much means that they aren't paying very close attention to the speech itself.

If you do not notice that some people fidget in this way, don't get diverted by that. You should maintain your focus on the things which you can control directly. If there are people who are giving off the signals of positivity, then try to feed off that energy. There will always be people who won't be all up in arms about the speech and it is necessary to accept this as an inevitability of the process.

How to Approach the Situation

Your approach is under your control. A strategy that is well put together can make or break certain speakers. Other speakers may prefer to play it by the ear without too much of a structure. Some people simply do better when they have notes while some like to keep the information contained in their mind since they find notes to be distracting and for those people notes can be a hindrance.

You need to be self-aware and have the knowledge of how you naturally interact with other people. If you are relaxed and spontaneous, then a short summary of the speech may work well for you since you find that you speak more naturally that way. Other people may prefer to have detailed plans and notes and that is perfectly fine. It is necessary to know what sort of approach will yield the best results for you specifically.

Whatever you do, you should always keep the audience in mind. Think about the speeches that have left a positive impression on you before. You can try to figure out what made those speeches so good so that you could mirror their success. You are naturally empathizing with the audience when you are doing things in this way.

Chapter 6: Tips & Tricks

It's never a bad idea to gather some tips and tricks about how to deal with the fear of public speaking. You can be more resourceful and you can work better with what you have this way. The best advice is usually very simple and very commonsensical. This sort of advice is easy to memorize and you can easily carry a reminder with those tips so that you never forget about them.

Everyone is different and therefore you will have to decide which tips will provide you with the best results personally. What may work great for you may not be as great for someone else. Just don't overthink things since you want to make taking the initial step as easy as you can.

How to Get Rid of Stress

Not being stressed is easier said than done and it is not actually entirely possible. What you should remember is that stress can be good. Instead of pushing against the stress, you can use it and benefit from it. It will take some time to assume this new perspective, but it will do you a lot of good if you can successfully adopt it.

You have probably heard countless times about the people who just tell you to not be stressed as if it were that easy. For most people, that simply doesn't work. The world would be a much happier place if it were so simple. Just focusing on stress can actually lead to anxiety since what you focus on expands.

Stress exists for a reason, just like fear. People need some stress to actually get anywhere. It is only necessary to worry if the burden of the stress becomes too overwhelming, and in that case, it is necessary to utilize certain techniques for managing and alleviating anxiety.

When you manage stress, you aren't letting it go. You can actually use it during your speech. If you know what to do with the release of stress, then you can end up bringing a lot of creativity to your speech.

How to Benefit from Nervous Energy

Stress should be looked at as energy which can be used in order to gain an advantage. You will find taking control of your anxiety to be very helpful and it will serve you a lot more than worrying about all the countless things which make you lose focus.

There are several ways in which this nervous energy can benefit you. By doing so you can create a personality around your public speaking which will allow you to deliver the message more effectively. For example, if you are not all that great at pausing and controlling the volume, then you can use the stress energy to focus on that.

You can improve your performance by knowing how to direct your nervous energy. As aways, some people will be naturals at this while others will need a bit more practice in order to accomplish the same thing.

You want to learn how to take advantage of stress instead of just letting it go. There is actually a great power there and it is a shame to let it go to waste just like that. Stress can serve a useful purpose and you can actually harness that energy. You can release the stress just by laughing. It is a lot better to use stress instead of just trying to rise above it. It is all about focusing on what you actually can control.

Be Aware of Your Limits

Everyone has their limits. You have to have good situational awareness if you plan to hold a presentation which will serve its purpose. A recommended way to deal with a public speaking occassion is to create realistic limits for yourself. You just have to keep reminding yourself that the audience is your ally and that they don't want to see you have a bad time since to them that is almost as bad as them having to deal with that themselves. In order to be within your limits, you want to make sure that your goals are reachable.

It is very good to have goals if you are using some form of exposure or desensitization therapy. It will be a lot easier for you if you have smaller milestones which should lead you to a large ultimate goal. It is way easier to learn anything if you can break it down into small manageable chunks. Your brain loves doing things that way. By just sticking to this process, you will learn a lot. You will recognize the fear and then you will be able to replace it with something a lot healthier.

Learning in small and manageable steps is a lot more realistic and manageable instead of taking huge leaps, regardless of the fact that taking huge leaps seems more glamorous. Everything is better than just jumping swiftly into a public speaking gig without having a strategy that is based on your limits. Just remember that huge goals can work against you and that realistic ones which you can achieve in your current state will work a lot better for you. Break down the whole undertaking of public speaking into small, manageable chunks first, you can make your goals larger later down the road.

Don't Get Stuck in Paralysis by Analysis

For anyone who is not a natural at public speaking, proper preparation is non-negotiable. Some people can naturally have hours of amazing stuff to say, but you don't need to go that far in order to get the job done as far as public speaking is concerned.

You shouldn't spend all your time preparing yourself since overdoing it with the rehearsing can work against you. You gotta realize that things are rarely going to play out perfectly and that distractions are always possible. Someone in the audience may not be on their best behavior, or you may lose your train of thought.

This is simply what you can expect when you are doing public speaking live. You could be sabotaging your chances of success by excessively preparing yourself for your public speaking event. You are aiming for perfection when you are rehearsing excessively and you may not be able to handle something unexpected. You should be ready for the unexpected.

You can also try to go way beyond your current level of capabilities when you overprepare. You may try to do too many things in not that much time which could result in blandness all across the board and you spreading yourself too thin.

Rehearsing is important, but it should be done in moderation. If you start thinking that you are overpreparing, then that is likely the case. You want to know which information in the presentation is essential and you want to stick to that instead of packing way too much filler in your presentation. Make sure that you really understand the material so that you wouldn't completely rely on memorization.

Chapter 7: Reliable Public Speaking Techniques

You Can't Go Wrong With Humor

Stress is released with laughter and anyone can benefit from that. You are not the only one under stress during the presentation, there is a chance that the audience is feeling quite similar. That is why it is necessary to create a warm, inclusive atmosphere which will lend itself well to some humor.

You don't need to be a stand-up comedian in order to make this work, it is enough if you use a bit of humor to harness your nervous energy in order to deliver it. You can't go wrong by adopting a lighthearted persona for the occasion.

You don't want to come across as trying too hard to be funny. Comedy is all about timing if you want to make it work well. You should design your whole approach so that the audience doesn't get the impression that they are in a comedy show. You don't have to go overboard, you just have to make sure that the presentation is warm and energetic and that there is an atmosphere of friendliness.

You can't possibly control entirely how your audience will respond and laughter shouldn't be your goal every time. What should be your focus is making sure that you and your audience are comfortable and this is done with smiling, eye contact and anything that would harness nervous energy in a productive manner.

How To Ensure That Everyone Gets What They Want

When you come across as a warm person who actually cares, you are making sure that both you and your audience win. There are a lot of things that tend to happen to every public speaker which would be viewed as an obstacle by most people. However, it is possible to take this obstacle and to turn them into an advantage.

One possible obstacle is the silent pause and this can cause many people to become anxious. It doesn't have to be that way. A pause which is intentional can do a lot for the presentation if someone knows how to time it. A good pause gives an audience an opportunity and a time to think about and to process what is being presented. The pause also gives you, as a presenter, an opportunity to figure out what is next.

Not every pause will happen perfectly according to plan and some will simply be a result of an accident. It is necessary not to panic and not to become paralyzed by fear which would only make this unnecessary pause harder to overcome. Some silence is inevitable and it is up to you how you will handle it.

If you want to have a method which you can use to get yourself out of the awkward scenario, you can simply repeat your last sentence with a stronger emphasis which should give you enough time to recollect so that you could move on. You can sprinkle some humor in order to shift the dynamic of the situation back to the positivity.

At the end of the day, you just have to remind yourself that nothing bad can happen and that there is nothing to worry about. The best thing to do is to see inconveniences such as silences as what they are, an opportunity to refocus and to move forward. You can create a scenario in which everyone can win by just learning to look at obstacles as opportunities.

How to Deal With Mistakes

Mistakes are unavoidable on the road to becoming a good public speaker. Only robots have a chance of doing things perfectly according to plan without mistakes, but people simply don't relate to robots. People will find it easier to relate if they see some flaws.

For example, a certain presenter may ask for a moment in order to recollect the thoughts. When the presenter regains control of the situation, then he or she can follow this up by thanking the audience for their patience and understanding. Something like this could be planned out as well, but it would make the presenter come across as more genuine either way.

As long as the presenter remains honest and warm during the presentation as a whole, the audience will barely register a slight mistake here and there. These situations can be really turned around by adding in some humor at such a moment.

The Power of Being Humble

People are universally drawn to the displays of humility. People in the audience actually want to relate to the speaker somewhat. An atmosphere of warmth and compassion aren't necessarily created by loud and pretentious personalities. However, this doesn't mean that anyone can just simply be themselves and call it a day.

You can form a personality specifically for your public speaking occasions. You don't necessarily have to reveal yourself as you truly are. This may sound manipulative, but most public speakers you admire actually create a personality specifically for their public speaking events.

Even if you have a lot of knowledge about a certain topic, it could still be a good idea to create a persona which would downplay that a knowledge a bit so that the whole situation would be more relatable to the audience unlike the situation involving a perfect, all-knowing presenter who never makes mistakes.

Purposeful Speaking

Your performance can be much better if there is a clear purpose behind it and if you believe in that purpose. The audience will pick up the fact that you don't really care about the information if that happens to be the case. You can make any topic engaging and interesting if there is a clear purpose behind it.

Your message should contain some value, but it can be hard to convey that if someone is way too caught up in worrying about their fears or about how they are being perceived. There won't be many issues you will have to worry about if there is a clear purpose behind the speech and if you are aware of that purpose.

It will be much easier to create a passion driven presentation when you have a clear purpose. It is necessary for a presentation to provide value before an attempt is made to inform or influence someone. Doing this can be difficult, but it can really pay off. For example, you may think that the reason for a holding a certain speech isn't significant enough. However, the speech itself is obviously important for some reason. If you can figure out that reason, you will find it much easier to create a value driven and purposeful presentation.

The Power of Focusing on Less

A little information, as long as it is selected carefully, can be really impactful. You rarely need to focus on more than a couple of key points which are backed up by evidence and filler.

When you are creating a presentation, you want to make it easier for the audience to commit key points to memory. It is the fact that people, in most cases, don't remember public speaking events entirely since processing auditory information can be overwhelming, especially if there is a lot of information. You always want to keep your purpose in mind so that you could keep the presentation concise. You don't need to have more than three or four key points in order to achieve this.

Your overall presentation can be negatively affected by too many information and details since that can create a burden. In the case of the audience being confused about the purpose of the presentation, they would have to sort through the information to separate the important from the unimportant and that is why it is helpful to have less key points.

You as a speaker will also be more stressed if you try to cram way too much information into a speech. Give yourself some space because by doing so you are allowing your audience to take in the information. Your audience will be more focused and will remember more if you make sure to have fewer key points.

Choosing the Right Words

Choosing the right words can really make a difference since that will add more soul to a speech. There is a lot of truth in this. You can't go wrong with clear and concise words which anyone can understand without ambiguity. Your audience will remember the presentation much more fondly if the content of the presentation is focused.

People don't like boring lectures and they will have a lot more appreciation for a brief delivery which has a good blend of pauses and emphasis. You are in the control of your key points and how you present them and your ability to do so well will have an impact on the experience of the audience.

How to Perceive Yourself

Your self-perception is something that is worth your attention. You don't want to consider yourself to be a public speaker because there isn't much use in comparing yourself to other presenters. You should develop your own style whether that means being authentic or having a persona specific to public speaking.

You don't necessarily have to be a public speaking star in order to get your point across effectively. The audience is something you should always be aware of so that you could deliver your message in the most effective way possible. You will just get discouraged by huge expectations if you perceive yourself as a public speaker since you will never feel like you are good enough.

The presentation should always be about the core purpose instead of being about yourself. You will just waste time and energy by worrying about how you are perceived by others since this is something you can't control directly. You should view yourself as a messenger with a role of getting an important message out to people.

Chapter 8: How to Gain Support

It will be very hard to rise above the fear of public speaking without having some kind of support from others. A lot of different groups of people can support you on your way to beating the fear of public speaking. Friends and family can help you a lot and there are also groups which are specifically designed to help people who deal with exactly the same fears and anxieties related to public speaking.

Just make sure that you are aware of all the options that you have at hand. Some people will get the best results through hypnosis. Other people will benefit more from a Toastmasters group. Taking part in public speaking classes can benefit you a lot. For the most people, working with friends and family to rise above the fear of public speaking will be the first choice.

Support From Friends and Family

A great way to get started with public speaking is to practice with a group of friends or with family. If you want to gradually expose yourself to the crowd, it is best to do so in a safe and controlled environment. This will take some practice, but you will inevitably become more comfortable with public speaking if you keep at it.

That is essentially what exposure therapy and desensitization are all about. It is about making you realize that you are safe. The practice is much easier if you don't have to concern yourself with judgment. Try to be less of a perfectionist in order to reduce some pressure from the whole situation.

Take your time when choosing your audience. This will work the best if your friends and family provide you with honest feedback and they will do so as long as they are interested in you succeeding. This is how you find out if you know how to speak with purpose. Good feedback should address the key points of your presentation.

Public Speaking Courses

Not everyone will be thrilled with the prospect of taking a public speaking class and they may prefer going to a dentist over a public speaking class. The fact is that the same people who take these classes have the same fear and anxiety as you do. If someone can rise above these fears, then a lot can be gained from these classes.

Public speaking classes can provide you with all kinds of techniques you can use to improve your speeches and your confidence overall. These techniques can also help you get over your fear.

The best approach is to focus on the purpose of the speech and the techniques instead of how you are being perceived by others. There is a personalized element to these classes and you can be helped with finding out which approach will provide you with the best results. The right choice of approach will ensure that you can keep your composure and not get emotional.

Using Hypnosis

Another tool you could benefit from is hypnosis. Fears are ingrained deeply into how you think and how you physically react during fearful circumstances. Hypnosis can make overcoming the fear of public speaking that much quicker and it can act as a shortcut.

However, not everyone requires hypnosis and whether it is necessary, should be decided by a health care professional. Most common hypnosis techniques which could be utilized by professionals are visualization and relaxation. If someone can't let go of their fears, then those approaches are a good idea.

Toastmasters

It won't be easy to find a better resource than Toastmasters International for getting over the fear of public speaking. The Organization features numerous services and support which have the ultimate purpose of helping you get over the fear of public speaking.

Everyone is different and that is why a lot of information and resources are tailored towards individual's s specific needs. It's hard to not get something out of Toastmasters International. Even those who don't necessarily have to deal with the fear of public speaking can gain something from what is offered by Toastmasters.

The information which is provided can range from tips for beginners to inspiring stories which can help you get over your fears. The organization creates an atmosphere of belonging for everyone, no matter where they may be in terms of their speaking abilities.

Chapter 9: How to Get Started

It can be a lot easier to overcome the anxiety of speaking in public if you are aware of what fear of public speaking entails. It really helps if you are aware of the severity of your fear before getting started. You can start taking action once you are aware of where you are with your fear.

You need to know how to evaluate your needs in order to succeed. Some people may benefit more from a cognitive approach while others may need to consult a professional such as a physician or a hypnotist. You are not alone when it comes to the fear of public speaking. A lot of people are dealing with the same thing when it comes to how they react emotionally and physically. There are a lot of good reasons for taking action in handling the fear of public speaking. There are also a whole lot of stories which can be used for inspiration and encouragement.

Most importantly of all, you have to apply the theory since knowledge is only potential power. Just knowing what to do isn't enough. You will get over your fears as long as you regularly apply the techniques and approaches. An approach you will undertake should be tailored to you specifically.

Fears and Phobias

Fear is a natural response to certain things and circumstances and it plays an important role in making self-preservation possible for people. It may seem like the fear of public speaking doesn't make sense, but it isn't so unreasonable when you consider how it may feel standing and facing the crowd head-on.

A phobia is a fear which is excessive and which can prevent a person to go about everyday life normally. Some people may have a phobia of speaking in public, which is also referred to as glossophobia, and this may be behind some of the other fear of that person.

Know What You Are Dealing With

Fear is a strong emotion and it may be tricky to figure out if someone is dealing with a simple case of stage fright or if glossophobia is in question. There are ways in which you can determine the severity of your condition.

If you are finding it difficult to go normally through your day without being anxious about a chance of speaking in public, then it may be recommended to consult a professional. Phobias can be treated very effectively and the treatment can surpass someone's expectation with how well it works.

Know What You Need

Everyone's situation is different since everyone has different experiences and memories which means that the extent to which people are scared varies. The best approach is to start small and simple and to visualize your speech in front of a small group of people. Pay attention to whether that scenario is easy or overwhelming for you.

Some people may require a professional approach such as therapy while some will use medications if their situation is more severe. Certain medicines can effectively inhibit how someone responds to fear so that the situation could be handled in a more controlled manner.

Other people may find that utilizing a cognitive approach could help them be more rational towards public speaking instead of being emotional. Others may benefit the most by collaborating with other people in a public speaking class or with some other group such as family and friends.

For most people, Toastmasters International can be a great resource to deal with the fear of speaking in public. Toastmasters organizations is all about helping people with this fear and this fear specifically.

A Universal Issue

Bravery isn't the absence of fear. Bravery lies in the ability to overcome fears. There aren't many people who don't feel the fear of public speaking. This feeling is pretty natural and to be brave, you have to know how to control this fear.

Reactions to Public Speaking

Emotional and bodily responses to speaking in public aren't anything unnatural although the extent of the reaction varies from individual to individual. Some reactions such as dry mouth and shallow breathing can be expected as a part of the public speaking experience. These reactions will be there most of the time and it would be useful to know how to use them.

All of those reactions are a form of energy and that energy can be channeled positively as you deliver your speech. This nervous energy can be your tool if you know what to do with it.

The Audience is Your Friend

The fear of public speaking simply comes with being human and that is why some sympathy can be expected from an audience every time you are in a public speaking situation. Almost anyone can relate to this fear, and that is why it is helpful to view the audience as an ally instead of viewing it as an obstacle.

There is a reason why your audience is attending a speech. A speech has to have a purpose. Fears tend to diminish when the focus is placed on what an audience needs and why they are there.

In order to work better with your audience, you could include some humor and humility into the presentation. The audience is likely to be aware of your fear about the whole situation and the fact that simply going through with the speech requires bravery. If you see certain audience members return to following speeches, then you know you are doing something right.

How you perceive yourself and the situation is powerful. If someone goes into public speaking thinking that they have to have extraordinary talent and wits, then they are more likely to suffer from overwhelm. The easy self-perception tip to follow is to see yourself as a purpose driven individual.

There is an invisible flow of energy between the presenter and the audience. Things that tend to make people nervous can be turned around in the speaker's favor if fear is recognized as excitement. Recognizing that the speaker and the audience are in the whole thing together really helps.

177

Conclusion of Public Speaking Fear

The fear of public speaking can be overcome by reengineering your perception of yourself. The ideal way to perceive yourself is a crucial part of the audience instead of as a speaker who is facing an audience. A speaker acts as an extension of what the audience is hoping to get out of the presentation.

In order to get over any fear, practice is necessary. Which approach will be utilized will depend on the severity of the fear. Everyone has uniques experiences and the best results will be gained by adopting an approached which is personalized towards an individual.

Just having the knowledge isn't enough and just sitting on that knowledge will produce little in terms of results. It requires action to apply the knowledge after the ideal course of action was established for the individual.

It's best to start off small and it is best to start the practical application with something as simple as imagining giving a speech to the audience. The size of the audience can be whichever size someone is comfortable with. Someone can easily determine if they are dealing with a fear or a phobia by taking the first step such as this one.

The framing of the situation changes how the situation is seen. If someone can see the situation for what it is, then it is easier to approach a task in an objective manner by adopting a cognitive approach. This can only be successfully achieved through practice and through a commitment to mastering the responses towards public speaking.

An easy way to practice speaking is to have one idea which the speech is centered around. Getting the point across clearly should be the main goal. You can also practice by utilizing pauses to add emphasis since you won't do as well with speeches by trying to fill every second with speaking and not embracing the silence.

In order to be objective successfully, it is necessary to understand the origin of the fear within the brain. The brain is wired for the body to react automatically to certain stimuli. It is necessary to look at these responses objectively and to accept that they are the part of the whole ordeal.

To really get a grip on your fear, make sure to use the tools and resources that are already at your disposal. Groups can be used, such as Toastmasters, in order to get good personalized information and a sense of belonging. Friends and family can also be used for support as long as they remain open and honest with how they react. Practicing in a safe environment around people who want to see you succeed is how you get to the root of your fear.

If it turns out that glossophobia is the real issue, then a professional should be consulted. Techniques and methods such as desensitization and exposure therapy can be used to help with that. Some people may benefit from hypnosis since the brain is rewired to respond to public speaking environment and situations in a healthier manner. Successful hypnosis can make the whole process go much quicker.

If you want to see progress, then you need a plan of action. If there is something you want to overcome, such as a stutter, then you need to dedicate yourself to the process of turning that around. You can overcome the fear of public speaking by practicing speaking about a topic you are passionate about, whatever that may be. You will always do better if you talk about your interests. This is only the beginning, presentations which are interesting no matter the subject can be created by someone skilled enough.

In order to attain the skill, it is necessary to practice, and practice comes in many variants. One example is reciting parts of your favorite book in a place where you are out of reach and where you won't be interrupted. To practice effectively, it is necessary to channel the nervous energy in positive ways. Practicing like this over time in combination with relaxation techniques will produce great results.

Some stress is to be expected when delivering a speech. The response to the stress is what is most important. Relaxation techniques will be different for each individual. The right approach for you is the one which will provide you with the perfect balance between anxiety and good performance. The audience can be imagined as a group of people who are there for good information. Doing this takes some pressure of the whole situation since you are positioning yourself merely as a messenger.

In order to succeed, it is important to familiarize yourself with the process. Practice does make perfect when it comes to public speaking. Whenever you do anything for the first time, it is unlikely to end up being great. Sometimes the task can be completed easily without much effort while in other cases you can struggle with no end in sight. No matter how much effort is required, tasks can be mastered if someone is persistent enough.

It is necessary to keep reminding yourself that it is possible to overcome the fear of public speaking and that the only thing that differentiates someone starting out and someone with inherent talent is the time it will take to reach the goal and the willingness to keep going. It all comes down to willingness since just because someone is talented, that doesn't mean that the person will do what it takes to reach their goal.

Stuttering

Help

A Guide to Simple Techniques Which You Can Use
to Control Your Stutter so That You Can Speak
Fluently and With Confidence

By Clark Darsey

Introduction to Stuttering Help

Stuttering is an uncomfortable issue. When you are not able to speak plainly, it affects each aspect of your life. It could hinder your relations with other individuals, and cause you to end up being secluded. You might be so ashamed by your speech that you talk as little as you can. You believe your speech is inadequate-- that you are not conveying your point.

If stuttering has actually been an issue for you, do not surrender hope-- there are options! You could discover how to take control of your speech, instead of enabling it to manage you!

There are lots of easy techniques to aid to manage your stuttering. When you go through all that you could do, you ought to begin to feel confident. When you attempt these techniques, you are going to discover which ones work ideally. From the convenience and personal privacy of your own home, you are going to find it really simple to learn these techniques. You could then start to use them in your daily speech to see how they work.

Even if you have actually stuttered for plenty of years, these simple techniques are going to end up being useful solutions to your stuttering. They are going to aid you to find out how to speak plainly and successfully. Speaking with individuals, in groups, and even publicly, could be as satisfying as it was supposed to be-- every single time without fail.

Mastering the simple techniques to manage your stutter could do marvels for your self-confidence. When you have found out the art of communicating properly, it is going to boost your self-confidence in your life.

Some individuals require a little extra assistance to manage their stuttering. Often there are unique circumstances that call for a special method in order to work. Whatever category describes you, they are all dealt with here within this book and you are bound to find something for you.

Chapter 1: You Can Utilize Simple Techniques to Manage Stuttering

For the majority of people who stutter, mastering some fundamental techniques is all they have to do. Stuttering does not need to ever be an issue again. All it requires is the dedication to attempt these techniques, and discover which ones work ideally. You might discover that you have to utilize a variety of methods so as to have effective speech. With a bit of practice, they are going to come naturally. You could anticipate a lifetime of talking confidently!

There are 2 essential points to bear in mind before you attempt these methods, and as you are practicing them. Initially, there is no one technique that works similarly well for everybody. This is why there are numerous techniques noted here. You have to attempt all of them to discover which ones work ideally for you.

Second, whether your stuttering is minor or severe, you can not acquire ideal, perfect control over stuttering overnight. It requires effort and practice on your end, and it requires time for you to see the outcomes. If you want to make this dedication and do not expect your stutter to vanish in a day, you are going to have the ability to find out which of these methods works for you. Your speech is going to no longer be a reason for shame or concern-- it could be among the most satisfying aspects of your life!

Chapter 2: Think About What You Want to Communicate

There is a lot more to speech than just speaking words. When you speak with somebody, you are trying to convey a thing. Possibly you are attempting to get the point across, clarify something or ask a question. Whenever you talk, you are trying to convey a message. Considering what you want to communicate beforehand has advantages that can aid you to manage your stuttering.

The message you want to offer has its own tone. It includes your state of mind, your mindset, your thoughts and feelings-- a lot more than simply words! What do you wish to say, and what do you hope the listener is going to get from it? It just takes a couple of minutes to think about these aspects before you start to speak.

Thinking of what you wish to communicate puts strength into your message. It could additionally put strength into your speech. The way this is performed is it places your focus on the significance of what you are saying-- why it is crucial. This focus could, consequently, shift your self-consciousness far from your talking. It might even get rid of it completely.

Rather than just saying words, which you might stumble on, you are going to be communicating your state of mind, mindset, and confidence, which accompanies it. You are going to be speaking plainly, instead of guarding your speech. With practice, this technique could aid you to manage your stutter.

Chapter 3: Eye Contact

The individual who stutters typically establishes the routine of avoiding eye contact with individuals to whom he is speaking. He has actually ended up being so adapted to his faltering speech that he does not wish to see the response of the listener. This could induce you to end up being a lot more uneasy and stutter a lot more.

You could turn this unfavorable habit around. While it might require a bit of practice, it is well worth it. When you are getting ready to talk to somebody, make sure to make eye contact with that person. You could start by reminding yourself that he truly does wish to hear whatever you intend to say. For the most part, you are going to get a unspoken or spoken affirmation of this, before you start to talk.

As you talk, maintain eye contact with the individual. If you talk nicely and show this pleasant mindset in the eye contact instead of a vibrant gaze, you are going to see that he is listening enthusiastically to whatever you are talking about.

This method could aid you to establish the practice of valuing one-on-one interaction. It could aid you to concentrate on the interaction itself, rather than on your speech difficulty. You are going to acquire control over your verbal communications, and discover them to be a lot more satisfying. As these habits begin to come naturally, your speech is going to additionally start to stream more naturally.

Chapter 4: Deep Breathing

Appropriate breathing could have a considerable role in managing your stutter. It is an excellent, healthy practice that you could start doing by yourself and place it into practical use.

You could start by learning deep breathing on your own, in the privacy of your own house. Begin by taking deep, slow breaths, breathing in intentionally, and after that, breathing out just as slowly. Doing this in a calm, peaceful environment where you are not going to be disrupted by other individuals or outdoor noise is preferable. The less diversions you have, the better. Practice this simple, deep breathing method one or two times a day-- however long you require for it to feel natural like you have been doing it forever.

If you want, you could include a bit of rehearsal after you have actually found out to do this. It could increase your confidence in case you practice this brand-new technique on an your pet or an object. While this might sound uncommon, you might be shocked at how effective it can be! You could rehearse by incorporating this deep breathing method before, and throughout, your "conversation" with your pet. Do the deep breathing method prior to starting to talk and shortly throughout your "conversation."

Deep breathing throughout speech gives a variety of advantages. Initially, when your focus is taken off your speech and concentrated on your breathing, you are going to be more self-assured when you are talking. Additionally, deep breathing readies your body for a smooth, successful speech. It unwinds all of the muscles which you utilize as you are talking, aiding your speech to stream effortlessly.

After you have actually found out to do this, you could test it on another individual. It is necessary to remember that after you have learned this practice, the individual you are talking to is going to most likely not even realize you are doing it. Your speech is going to be more deliberate, well-thought, and with lower likelihood of stuttering.

Chapter 5: Establish an Excellent Sense of Humor

Stuttering is not funny. In case you stutter, you already understand this. Nevertheless, even when you start finding out how to manage your stutter, you might periodically make blunders. How you approach a mistake could make all the distinction in the world-- not just to that one specific conversation yet additionally in how you go towards future conversations.

Having the ability to say "Oops!" and laugh at a blunder might not come effortlessly. This is particularly true if you have actually been mocked about your stuttering before. Nevertheless, a sense of humor regarding your stutter is the healthiest approach to establish.

Establishing a sense of humor regarding your stutter is a thing ideally started when you are by yourself while no one else is watching. Consider circumstances you have actually been in, when your stutter was especially irritating. Think about just how much better the ultimate result might have been if you had actually had the ability to laugh and make a joke out of it. It would not have appeared so terrible if it was handled properly.

Next, consider how you could integrate humor into stuttering in the future. Possibly you could think of it in identical terms as an unscripted bout of hiccups. If a hiccup would not lead you to end up being ashamed and flustered, neither should a stutter. Be ready for such situations because they will come inevitably.

Understanding that you are going to commit mistakes is the ideal method to be ready for them. Actually, recognizing the chance of a mistake makes it less probable for one to, in fact, happen. You recognize that you aren't able to be perfect, and you are ready for what to do when you are not. You are not going to stress over stuttering, and verbal interaction are going to be a lot more pleasurable for yourself and for everybody else involved.

Chapter 6: Calm Yourself

If you remember your stuttering history, you might see just how big of an issue it was whenever you were nervous. If you are nervous, you end up being awkward; when you are awkward, you aren't really in control. It could end up being a vicious cycle of uneasiness, inhibition, and loss of control.

Keeping your calm requires practice and work. In case you are naturally nervous, or if your daily life frequently consists of scenarios that provoke uneasiness, it might require additional effort.

The calmer you have the ability to remain on a routine basis, the more control you are going to have when it comes to your stutter. As stammering and stuttering could be directly related to uneasiness, working on this issue could minimize your stuttering and provide you with more control. Teaching yourself to embrace a calm disposition and a positive outlook might not get rid of your stuttering, however, it could aid to lower it.

Along with these elements, particular products that you consume could additionally contribute to uneasiness. Caffeine is among the most frequent offenders. If you have the habit of consuming numerous servings of tea, coffee, or sodas throughout the day, switching to healthier, non-caffeinated drinks might be valuable. The restlessness that you feel after consuming a big amount of caffeine could impact each part of your body, involving the muscles that are utilized throughout the speech. Giving up this product, or at least reducing your usage of it, might be advantageous.

Certain individuals have a comparable response to sugar. While this is not correct for everybody, it deserves examining if you have a stuttering issue. Decreasing the sugar in your diet might aid you to end up being calmer. You could attempt it and see if it helps!

Chapter 7: Is Avoidance a Useful Strategy?

When it pertains to the topic of stuttering, certain techniques are really useful to some individuals, while not as helpful for others. This is since every person is an individual, and everyone's stuttering issue is distinct to him or her. The only method to understand for certain which methods are going to work for you is to offer them all a shot and see what works for you.

Avoidance is a controversial problem. Certain individuals claim it works rather well, while others do not find it as handy. The controversy is in whether avoidance is a suitable method for managing a stuttering issue. If you are serious about discovering techniques which work, it is an excellent idea to overlook that whole controversy and test it for yourself and see what you make of it.

The standard manner in which avoidance is practiced is to place words which are simple to speak instead of those that are not so simple to speak. If you have actually been bothered by your stuttering to the extent of checking out this guide, you are most likely already aware of the distinction.

You have seen that numerous words appear to stream rather effortlessly, while others end up being "stuck" or repeat. You might have additionally observed that particular sounds, or particular alphabet letters, are more annoying than others.

When you are thinking about this method, you might want to take a look at both sides of the problem. This could aid you to choose whether it is appropriate for you, and what you might be handling when you attempt it. Initially, practicing avoidance could aid you to feel generally more in control of your talking. When you understand what you want to say, and how you intend to say it, it could offer you a decided benefit. Rather than questioning and stressing, you are going to remain in control.

Nevertheless, avoidance could additionally have unfavorable ramifications. As you approach talking to somebody in this way, you might end up being more uncomfortable. For certain individuals, this could backfire; for others, it is not an issue whatsoever.

If you want to give this method a shot, put a bit of time into the "demons" of your talking. When you understand what words, letters and sounds are usually at fault for creating a stutter, you could select a different word which means the same thing. You are going to discover that language is a lovely thing without a doubt-- there is a synonym, or a related word, for each word you wish to say! For instance, if the word "box" is among your speech demons, attempt saying "container" as an alternative. You could expand your vocabulary, while learning a new method by which to manage your stutter.

Chapter 8: Establish the Habit of Slowly Talking

You might already understand that as your words come out in an out of breath rush, your stutter ends up being worse. You begin to say a word, and numerous other words appear to tumble after, as a domino-effect. Establishing the habit of slowly speaking is a method that could assist you in managing your stutter.

Knowing how to talk slowly is not really hard. If you have actually not yet cultivated this habit, now is a great time to start. When you wish to speak, take a minute to prepare yourself. Create each word gradually, and make it possible for every word to stream naturally and smoothly. Instead of remaining in a rush to get a total sentence out, consider every word as streaming from you to the other person.

When you discover that the other individual is listening to what you are saying, this could aid you to talk gradually. Interaction is supposed to be a favorable experience. It is far more than just exchanging words, or waiting for your opportunity to talk. It is among the ideal methods to delight in and value the company of another individual-- by exchanging ideas, feelings, thoughts, and information. Having these concepts at the base of your verbal interaction could be considerably helpful in having it in perspective.

This point of view can additionally help you in discovering how to talk slowly. You do not have to get your words out rapidly since the other individual is listening and appreciates all the things you say! He/she is genuinely interested! When you think of it in this manner, it ought to provide you with a reason to stop for a minute and think. You might be valuing your verbal interactions much more. Equally crucial, if you consider this when you are getting ready to have a conversation with somebody, it could aid you to manage your stutter. As your words stream smoothly and gradually, you are going to see how it helps your speech.

Chapter 9: How Relaxation Could Aid You to Manage Your Stutter

Relaxation has a dual function in managing stuttering. It works on both the mind and the body simultaneously. You might not have actually considered this prior, and you might not know of the numerous favorable impacts relaxation could have on you and your wellbeing.

Initially, relaxation impacts each part of your body-- your whole system. This consists of all of the muscles which are utilized as you speak. From the muscles in your throat to that fantastic diaphragm, the more relaxed your body is, the easier the words are going to stream. Relaxed muscles imply smoother speech; and smoother speech implies smaller likelihood of stuttering.

Next, relaxation impacts the mind. Even if you currently understand this, you might not have thought of how it is linked to your talking. The mind which is relaxed is more controlled and better focused. It is less troubled by little inconveniences, which produce uneasiness, stress, and self-consciousness. Consequently, when the mind is at ease and unwinded, you are less probable to experience serious stuttering.

How do you discover how to unwind, to ensure that you are able to enjoy these benefits? It is not tough, even if you have a hectic pace or lifestyle in which it seems that everything will collapse if you stop. You can start with deep, slow breathing. Imagine yourself in a wonderful, calm environment, where all the things are tranquil and serene. Permit yourself the luxury of dwelling in these types of thoughts occasionally, during the day.

After you have actually discovered how to do this, you could take this brand-new practice with you when you have to interact with other individuals. Before you start to talk, picture your calm atmosphere. Let the soothing relaxation to fill your body and mind. Not just is it going to feel more comfortable, even in social or business circumstances, you actually are going to be more at ease. Your body and mind are going to appreciate the impacts of relaxation and are going to aid you in managing your stutter.

Chapter 10: Establish Self-confidence in Your Talking

The more confidence you have, the less difficulty you are going to have with stuttering. This consists of confidence in yourself, along with self-confidence in your talking. If you have actually been troubled by stuttering for a while, it might require effort and time to establish this self-confidence. The rewards are going to be worth the effort you invest in it.

The more deserving and important you understand you are as an individual, the easier it is going to be to establish self-confidence in yourself. You could start by telling yourself that whatever you intend to state is crucial and that your listeners wish to hear from you. Even if you are shy naturally, this could aid you to end up being more assertive. When you go into the habit of showing a positive mindset, it is going to begin to boost the self-confidence you have. You are going to quickly see other individuals reacting in a favorable manner to the brand-new you!

Establishing self-confidence in your speech could be just as effortless. It demands a bit of practice, naturally, however discovering how to do it is rather straightforward. You could even start to apply self-confidence to your speech before you actually have it. This implies that even if you are not yet certain of yourself. When you talk as if you are sure about your capabilities, it is going to come true.

Self-confidence in speaking suggests beginning whatever you want to say as plainly and concisely as you can. Tell yourself that you are well-informed about the topic you are discussing and that it is necessary for you to say it. This sensation of authority is going to make you confident about what you are talking about. Allow your words to stream effortlessly, with the identical dash of authority and self-confidence. Let your words advance naturally, one at a time. While practicing the breathing method, you have actually already found out how to talk without stopping to pause on singular words.

When you have actually established this sort of self-confidence, you are going to be less probable to trip up on those frustrating words. With practice, your stutter might end up being a distant memory.

Chapter 11: Analyzing

You might have heard of analyzing. You might have attempted it yourself. The truth is that in numerous instances, it could aggravate stuttering. While this guide is supplying you with practical methods that could aid you in managing your stutter, it ought to be kept in mind that this frequent technique is seldom in best interest of a stutterer.

Analyzing is typically performed by putting effort and time into attempting to determine the issue, in the hope of alleviating it. Analyzing could consist of studying the vocabulary one regularly uses, looking for those pesky "demon" words. It could additionally consist of taking special note of the parts of one's body and muscles one utilizes throughout the daily speech.

The unfavorable element of analyzing in this way is it highlights the issue, instead of constructive solutions. You might find yourself so mindful of problematic words that it boosts the stuttering. You might end up being so concentrated on your muscles that it, in fact, impedes your capability to speak plainly. You could end up being so uneasy that your stuttering gets worse.

You are currently knowledgeable about the issue. Besides, you have actually been dealing with it for a while. Your objective ought to be to gain control of your stutter so that you could be pleased with your capability to communicate successfully. Putting an excessive focus on your stutter is not the ideal method to continue. Rather, recognizing that your issue could be conquered and that you can do it, is going to yield more successful outcomes. Instead of living in the issue, you are going to be living in the solution-- making the most of your spoken interactions.

Chapter 12: a Tip from a Celebrity

Based upon your interest in country music and age, you might be familiar with Mel Tillis. He has actually been among the most well-known country music singers throughout the previous couple of decades. A truth that many individuals do not recognize is that Mel Tillis has had difficulty with stuttering during his lifetime!

Mel Tillis has offered interviews before, mentioning that while his speech consists of stuttering, it is not there the moment he sings. Not just has this assisted him to establish self-confidence, it aided him to turn into one of the most beloved country music singers.

You may want to give this a shot, too. You could begin with one of your favorite singers, somebody of your gender whose voice resembles your own. Buy one of the person's CD's, and accompany him or her throughout songs you enjoy. After you have ended up being familiar with your singing voice, you might feel ready to sing along.

You might discover that your singing voice is as stunning, clear and stutter-free, as Mel Tillis's voice. This could be a terrific method to boost your self-confidence. The abler you are to sing without that obvious stutter, the more confident you are going to be in your routine verbal speaking.

This is an enjoyable method to gain control of your stutter. While the other methods call for practice, effort and work, you are going to certainly find this technique to be more satisfying. You might even establish a new pastime. You may not become a star such as Mel Tillis, however, you could take a suggestion from him to find out how to manage your stutter.

Chapter 13: Could Medication Be Useful?

You might be at wit's end with your stuttering. Maybe you have attempted these or other techniques and discovered that absolutely nothing works as effectively as you had wished. Maybe aggravation, fear, or concern is getting in the way of managing your stutter. You might be questioning if meds could fix the issue, or at the very least, alleviate it.

An excellent guideline is to rule out medication unless your stuttering is so serious that natural methods do not aid. While some individuals may disagree, utilizing any kind of meds for stuttering ought to just be considered as a last option. Unless your stuttering is being brought on by a medical issue that requires your physician's assessment and suggestions, depending on natural techniques is much better than depending on pharmaceuticals.

If you are thinking about medication, it is important for you to seek your doctor's guidance. Under no circumstances should you ever try to self-medicate. Utilizing any sort of pharmaceutical item without your physician's approval could be extremely harmful. Additionally, home remedies and devices ought to additionally be avoided. You desire alleviation from your stutter, however taking chances with your health is never ever the best option.

This chapter is going to offer you a summary of the medications that are typically utilized to alleviate or manage stuttering. Numerous physicians agree that their usage for this goal is extremely questionable. If you are considering attempting meds to manage your stutter, just your own physician could suggest a medication.

Zyprexa has a mild success rate in dealing with stuttering. This drug is mainly utilized for dealing with schizophrenia and other comparable issues. The experiences of individuals who have actually utilized Zyprexa for stuttering range from a high degree of satisfaction with the outcomes to little impact whatsoever. Zyprexa is a dopamine-blocker drug. Its side effects could vary from decreasing awareness to gaining weight.

There are a variety of medical conditions that contraindicate the use of Zyprexa, so it must never ever be utilized without your doctor having a complete understanding of your medical history. A lesser-known reality about Zyprexa is that its tablet kind consists of aspartame, making it hazardous for people who have phenylketonuria (typically called PKU).

While certain doctors disagree with the practice of prescribing tranquilizers as a remedy for stuttering, others think that they could be helpful. The overall consensus among those who consider it a proper form of treatment is that decreasing the individual's anxiety and uneasiness is going to, consequently, decrease his stuttering.

Even though the possible side effects of tranquilizers could vary from slight to extreme, an additional element is their potential to cause addiction. Addiction to tranquilizers is frequent, and withdrawal from these drugs is frequently tough and agonizing. If your physician thinks that this is the appropriate type of treatment, your utilization of tranquilizers needs to be thoroughly and regularly tracked.

Certain doctors think that antidepressants can aid in alleviating stuttering. Studies had actually revealed that while some individuals do get alleviation from this type of treatment, others experience worse stuttering than they had prior to the treatment started. As is the problem with any pharmaceutical option, making use of antidepressants needs to be decided on a case-by-case basis. Even with your medical history there, your physician might not have the ability to identify beforehand whether these drugs are going to assist you or whether your stuttering is going to worsen.

There are a lot of various antidepressants out there. While the negative side effects of antidepressants could vary from sleep disruptions to sexual problems and others, the side effects an individual experiences from using antidepressants is mainly based upon his own individual system. They could vary from extremely slight to extreme. Certain individuals discover the side effects of antidepressants to be just reasonably irritating, while others consider the negative side effects more unbearable than the first issue.

Two drugs presently on the marketplace, which demonstrate a significant amount of promise in dealing with stuttering are Risperdal and Haldol. Both of these are dopamine-blockers. While they both have the capacity of inducing significant side-effects in certain patients, studies have actually revealed these medications to have up to a fifty-percent success rate when utilized to deal with stuttering.

Numerous doctors agree that dopamine-blocking drugs are the first choice when utilizing medication to deal with stuttering. Nevertheless, as this has actually not been in practice for very long, it is smart to think about the ramifications of this truth prior to becoming quick to have a go at medication. While choosing whether the possibility of attaining some alleviation from stuttering is worth running the risk of the variety of prospective side-effects while using a medication might be hard enough, the absence of existing information on prospective long-lasting side-effects could make this decision even tougher.

You want to remedy for your stutter. You might want to go to any lengths to be without the issue.

For the sake of both your long-term and short-term health, you must not be too swift to choose that medication is the response. As any pharmaceutical option has the chance to result in problems, you need to plainly evaluate both the advantages and the dangers. You need to look for the guidance of a qualified doctor additionally.

The most reasonable approach to utilizing the meds for the stuttering treatment is to consider it just as the last option. Unless all of the natural techniques for managing your stutter have actually fallen short, and you have actually discovered that your stuttering disrupts your life to the extent that you can not deal with it, medication ought to be stayed clear of.

This chapter has been featured in this guide since many individuals are quick to consider medication as an excellent, quick, miracle-cure. They do not recognize how hazardous medication could be to their health. Regrettably, some capable doctors additionally have the viewpoint that medication is the ideal strategy, without initially examining all of the options.

When you have all of these truths, you are going to be in the ideal position to decide what is proper for you. You do not have to put unneeded risks on your health so as to alleviate your stutter. Almost everybody can attain outcomes which they are pleased with, without turning to medication.

Chapter 14: Special Needs: Stuttering in Kids

You might have bought this guide in the hope of aiding your kid with a stuttering issue. While much of the methods explained in this guide are just as suitable for kids, the kid who stutters has special needs that additionally need to be attended to.

A youngster who stutters remains in a particularly vulnerable position. Whether he is a young kid or a teen, stuttering could have more impact on a kid than on an adult. When you take your kid's special requirements into consideration, the methods in this guide are going to be more valuable to him.

The most substantial impact stuttering has on a kid is in his relations with other individuals, particularly his peers. Kids of all ages are typically subjected to mock when they show any sort of issue that separates them from their peers. A speech issue such as stuttering could hinder a kid's capability to communicate with his peers. He might be targeted for bullying and ridicule.

This special issue can make it far tougher for the kid to make buddies. It could be in the way of healthy socializing. It is not unusual for a kid who stutters to end up being depressed and isolated. He might be afraid of simple interaction, and incredibly uneasy. His self-confidence can be much lower than that of a non-stuttering kid; he might establish an unfavorable opinion of himself. He might additionally worry about carrying his stuttering with him for the remainder of his life.

These problems are why stuttering needs to be dealt with as quickly as you recognize it in your kid. The quicker you start to aid him in managing his stutter, the better his general life quality is going be. Oftentimes, stuttering is rather visible long before a kid starts school. In other circumstances, it is not obvious until he is older.

Building your kid's self-confidence works together with aiding him to manage his stutter. While it ought to be apparent, parents and other grownups must never ever make the mistake of shaming a kid about his stuttering. The more of a problem you make about his stuttering, the worse he is going to feel about himself. This, consequently, could lead to his stuttering worsening. He might feel that he is to blame for his issue, and that is going to make it more intense.

While grownups might not be hurt by making a joke of stuttering, this is seldom the case for kids. Even the most well-meaning siblings could hamper a kid's progress in managing a stutter by joking. It is no laughing matter to the child who stutters. Jokes and sarcasm could be ravaging to the kid.

The kid who stutters has to understand that you and the other individuals in his life are encouraging. He has to understand that he is not rejected, nor looked down on, over his issue. He has to understand that he is accepted and liked, just as he is-- stuttering involved. This type of unconditional love and approval are going to offer a strong base for assisting him in managing his stutter without the kid seeing the issue as a reflection of himself.

Offering a calm environment is the ideal method to start helping your kid to manage his stutter. In instances of extremely young kids, much of the techniques explained in this guide could be presented as games. Rather than presenting a method as something that he needs to perform so as to conquer an issue, letting him see a method as enjoyable and pleasurable is going to produce the ideal outcomes

Teaching a kid methods to aid him in managing his stutter can be more unpleasant and discouraging for the adult than it is for the child. He might not be cooperative, or you might not see any apparent outcomes. It is vital that you do not end up being demanding, or push him to practice a method. It is additionally important for you to not communicate your disappointment when you believe a method is worthless. Both of these mistakes could rapidly backfire. They could cause him to quit.

Convincing your kid that discovering methods to manage his stutter is something that he, in fact, wishes to do is not as tough as it might seem. The majority of parents already have practice in encouraging their kids that particular things are a good idea. When methods for managing stuttering are presented in a light-hearted, enjoyable way, your child is going to generally comply just since he wishes to comply.

While a parent might believe that rewarding a kid for learning a method is a favorable approach, it frequently is not. If your kid ends up being acclimated to rewards, this could make it even tougher for him when he is not effective. He might even feel that he is being penalized for slipping up-- and for not being excellent. When finding out how to manage a stutter, mistakes are as prevalent in kids as they are in grownups. Merely allowing him understand that you are happy with his efforts, despite the outcomes, is far better than providing him with rewards. A kid is going to be eager to discover a brand-new ability when he realizes that his efforts are valued.

When parents see their kid stuttering, they frequently freak out. This could indicate rushing him to his pediatrician, making appointments with speech therapists, and even thinking about meds. You could spare both yourself and your kid from a great deal of unneeded irritation by not being too fast to conclude that he is going to be a lifelong stutterer without instant intervention.

The truth is that numerous kids stutter sometimes. Some really young kids stutter when they are at first finding out verbal abilities; others stutter when they are very nervous, exhausted, or feel overloaded. In the interest of your kid's psychological health, you ought to resist seeing these types of circumstances as potentially-serious issues. If you are your kid's primary caretaker, it should not be tough to figure out whether he is showing a speech impediment or whether it is simply a phase.

Talking about the issue of stuttering in kids additionally consists of the element of medication. As parents are frequently not well-informed about this, it needs to be kept in mind that some medications that are frequently provided to kids could cause them to stutter, even if they do not have a real speech issue.

Ritalin, which is typically prescribed for conditions such as ADD and ADHD, is among the greatest offenders. If you observe stuttering in a kid who is taking this or other meds, it must be brought to the attention of his physician. The medication might be the reason for his stuttering. If so, calibrating the dose or changing medications could get rid of his stuttering completely. Nevertheless, this must not be tried without your physician's recommendation.

The kid who stutters is just as ordinary as other kids. How he is treated in his daily life must highlight this truth. Even though stuttering could be hazardous to a kid's self-confidence and social development, it is not nearly as hazardous as making an issue of it. The kid who understands that he is accepted and loved precisely as he is, while being supplied with methods to aid him to manage his stutter in the most satisfying manner feasible, is the kid who is more than likely to be prosperous.

Chapter 15: Do You Need a Speech Therapist?

Whether you are trying to find aid for yourself or for your kid, you might be considering requesting help from a speech therapist. You might question if this is the right choice. There are several points to think about when choosing if you or your kid should go to a speech therapist.

One example in which speaking with a speech therapist is a legitimate method is if stuttering is so serious that it affects your functioning. If it is so severe that it is disruptive to your daily life, help from a specialist might be in order. Whether the stuttering has actually been a long-lasting issue, or whether its start has been unexpected, a speech therapist could be valuable.

A 2nd scenario is if all methods and approaches for managing your stutter have stopped working. Even though the methods explained in this guide are simple to learn and effective for many individuals, they might not be as helpful for you. If you have actually put your best effort into these methods, and have discovered no remedy for your stuttering, a visit to a speech therapist might be in your best interest.

Another scenario that makes seeking advice from a speech therapist a smart choice is if your stuttering is connected to any medical or mental cause. In these circumstances, managing your stutter by yourself might be unattainable. If a current medical or mental condition is discovered to be the source of your stutter, a speech therapist could guide you to the professional help which is suitable for you.

While seeking advice from a speech therapist is not needed for the majority of instances of youth or teen stuttering, there are scenarios in which it is the ideal strategy. The kid whose stutter is so serious that no methods offer any alleviation is among these circumstances.

The kid whose stutter puts an excessive burden on his daily life is another. For the most part, kids react to natural techniques along with grownups. Nevertheless, if they do not work for your kid, taking him to a speech therapist could be in his best interest.

The kid who declines to comply in finding out how to manage his stutter is another situation that needs a speech therapist. This does not suggest rushing to make an appointment as soon as your kid doesn't want to comply. You should expect certain degree of disinterest or boredom when showing these new ideas to him. The kid who refuses to cooperate whatsoever, shows anger or animosity at your efforts to aid, or strongly believes that absolutely nothing is going to work, could gain from a speech therapist. The child who shows mental issues related to his stutter could additionally gain from seeing a specialist. In these instances, his pediatrician or your family doctor could suggest a therapist who could aid him.

If you or your kid is going to be seeing a speech therapist, these visits must not be any more disruptive to daily life than needed. The kid who sees a therapist might resent putting his time into it, and might think that this course of action is an unfavorable reflection on himself. The ideal technique for handling these problems effectively is to present the visits in a favorable light. If he sees his speech therapist as a pal, and as a nice individual who really wishes to assist him, he can eagerly anticipate the visits and gain from them a lot more.

Speech therapists could be expensive. If this is a problem for you, you require all of the facts prior to making a dedication. You could check to see if your insurance is going to cover a speech therapist or ask if he/she is going to accept a sensible payment plan. The cost must not be the deciding factor in whether to look for assistance from a professional.

Your pediatrician or family physician is the ideal resource for finding a speech therapist. He understands your specific circumstance and could suggest the therapist who is proper for you. Do not be reluctant in requesting his guidance.

For the most part, stuttering could be managed just by discovering these simple methods and applying them to your daily speech. Nevertheless, if you or your kid are in one of these special scenarios, a professional speech therapist could be significantly helpful. The sooner you request assistance, the quicker you could get the stutter under control.

Chapter 16: Progress Instead of Perfection

When you are learning anything brand-new, success does not come immediately. Anticipating overnight outcomes, or perfection, is a formula for catastrophe. This is among the most crucial points to keep in mind when you are finding out how to manage your stutter.

Expecting too much, prematurely, or expecting that you are never going to stutter again, puts excessive pressure on yourself. With this approach, you might end up being incredibly dissuaded and irritated when you do not attain the outcomes you desire as swiftly as you had wished. This sort of frustration could lead you to stop before you get favorable outcomes. It could additionally cause you to see a mistake or a small obstacle as a complete failure. You want to stay away from this sort of pressure if you genuinely want to be successful!

When you think about finding out how to manage your stutter in regards to learning a brand-new skill, both the outcomes and your mindset will be much better. As getting to know anything brand-new requires practice, time, and even trial-and-error, this is additionally the case with finding out how to manage your stutter. Certain methods are going to work better for you than others; some methods are not going benefit you; and others are going to provide you with outstanding outcomes. If you want to make that dedication, you can attain success.

Patience is the needed key in finding out how to manage your stutter. You need to be willing to invest your time into learning a technique, and applying it to your daily exchanges. When you slip up, you need to have the ability to let it go without letting it bother you. This is how to make progress.

Progress is not a promise of perfection. Even after you have actually mastered a method and applied it, you might still experience a mistake. You might have felt that you were entirely devoid of your stutter, just to have it happen at the most bothersome time. Instead of ending up being flustered, or worrying that you have actually not achieved anything, lightheartedly brushing it off is a far better strategy. You might not be flawless, yet you are still successful!

The idea of "progress- not perfection" is a lot more legitimate for the kid who stutters. As kids are more naturally inclined to see a small obstacle or mistake as a total disaster, teaching him to see his achievements for how remarkable they are is the most useful approach.

You could start by instilling this principle before you begin to teach him the methods to manage his stutter. Nothing genuinely worthwhile was ever achieved overnight, and even in the ideal situations, mistakes do happen. When he is equipped with these ideas before he begins discovering the methods, he is ready for success and is going to value it each step along the way.

Stuttering does not have to have a big part in your life. It does not have to hinder your communications with other individuals, nor impact how you think of yourself. All it requires is effort, time, and dedication to learn these straightforward methods. When you see which methods work ideally for you, practicing them is going to offer you a brand-new, positive view of your capability to talk plainly in social scenarios. Applying them regularly when you communicate verbally with other individuals is going to provide you with more self-confidence than prior.

Knowing how to manage your stutter is your initial step to a better, more satisfying life. The more you practice, the more progress you are going to make-- and this is the ideal description of real success!

I hope that you enjoyed reading through this book and that you have found it useful. If you want to share your thoughts on this book, you can do so by leaving a review on the Amazon page. Have a great rest of the day.